Living Culture, Living Christ

On Becoming Fully Human

— ALAN M. SUGGATE —

Sacristy Press

Sacristy Press
PO Box 612, Durham, DH1 9HT

www.sacristy.co.uk

First published in 2022 by Sacristy Press, Durham

Copyright © Alan M. Suggate 2022
The moral rights of the author have been asserted.

All rights reserved, no part of this publication may be reproduced or transmitted in any form or by any means, electronic, mechanical photocopying, documentary, film or in any other format without prior written permission of the publisher.

Scripture quotations, unless otherwise stated, are from the Revised Standard Version of the Bible, copyright © 1946, 1952, and 1971 National Council of the Churches of Christ in the United States of America. Used by permission. All rights reserved worldwide.

Every reasonable effort has been made to trace the copyright holders of material reproduced in this book, but if any have been inadvertently overlooked the publisher would be glad to hear from them.

Sacristy Limited, registered in England & Wales, number 7565667

British Library Cataloguing-in-Publication Data
A catalogue record for the book is available from the British Library

ISBN 978-1-78959-243-6

The saying that wisdom is the fruit of experience is abundantly vindicated in Alan Suggate's passionate yet reasoned defence of an Anglican-inspired Christian humanism. Liturgically rooted and politically engaged, this book represents the fine distillation of a lifetime of reflection and points us with real insight to the kind of public theology urgently needed in modern Britain.

Robert Song
Professor of Theological Ethics, Durham University

With reflection honed by international experience and the judicious critique of unpredictable resources, Alan Suggate explores the bonds of shared and interdependent lives in the universe of co-creators in which we find ourselves. He writes a markedly "Anglican" theology attentive both to our "common good" and to the central importance of distinctively Trinitarian "common worship"—a much needed focus for both thought and action in our troublesome times.

Ann Loades CBE
Honorary Professor in the School of Divinity, University of St Andrews

The great strength of this book lies in its rare combination of concern for even one person deprived of name and life in an inhuman world, critical and constructive reflections on our culture, and deep commitment to holistic Christianity.

Alan Suggate persuasively retrieves a more humane way forward, and grounds it in concrete and integral living in Christ, which is valid not only in Britain but worldwide, including in my own country of South Korea, where the weak suffer severely from the ravages of capitalism shorn of values and any sense of transcendence.

Deuk-Hoon Park
*Visiting Lecturer of Christian Economic Ethics,
Nehemiah Institute for Christian Studies*

In remembrance of
"No-name"

"As you did it to one of the least of these my brothers and sisters, you did it to me." Matthew 25:40 (author's translation)

In *Murder on the Middle Passage: The Trial of Captain Kimber*, Nicholas Rogers tells how in 1791 John Kimber skippered the slave ship *Recovery* to West Africa. One of Kimber's victims was a girl in her early teens. On the voyage, she was raped, brutalized and flogged daily for refusing or being unable to dance to keep her muscles in trim and so preserve her price in the market. Soon she was struggling to walk, hampered by a crooked knee. Kimber had her strung up from the mizzenmast by the bad leg, then by the other leg, then by each arm. She crawled to the hatch, slithered down the ladder into the hold, convulsed and within four days she died.

William Wilberforce denounced Kimber in Parliament and had him prosecuted for murder before the High Court of Admiralty. The judge, Sir James Marriott, stopped the trial after five hours and directed the jury to find the accused not guilty. There was pressure on him from the slave trade, and he concluded that the charge of murder would not stick. He immediately charged the prosecution's witnesses with perjury, along with two members of Kimber's crew who had testified against him; one was convicted and sentenced to transportation. Kimber sued Wilberforce for damages and stalked him to intimidate him.

A very potent explanation for this verdict lies in the context. The revolution of Haitian slaves had begun in 1791, jeopardizing the future of the slave colonies across the Caribbean; the French Terror was gathering momentum and war with France loomed; and the slave trade was still a vital artery running through the British empire. The trial of Kimber was considered dangerous commercially, politically and strategically. Necessity outweighed any humanitarianism.

There is no record of the girl's name, her family or her story. She is referred to as "No-name". I dedicate this book to the remembrance of her.

Contents

Preface.. v
Introduction... 1

Part 1. Our Culture.. 17
Part 2. Western Christianity................................... 56
Part 3. The Liturgy.. 93
Part 4. The Faith.. 130

Epilogue 156
Appendix 1: Exclusion and Embrace 160
Appendix 2: "What more do you want from me?" 166
Bibliography 172
Index 179

Preface

A fascinating feature of a long life is the sheer wealth of experience that comes from living through many different phases of history. Born in the brief turbulent reign of Edward VIII, I lived right through the Second World War, from the blitz of my native city of Sheffield to the ghastly revelations of Belsen and Auschwitz, the rubble of great European cities and the atomic devastation of Hiroshima and Nagasaki. In the period from 1945 to 1979, there came first the great Attlee administration and the long years of slow recovery; the dismantling of our empire; the joy of the coronation; growing material prosperity and the swinging sixties; and then the strife of the seventies and our joining the European Economic Community. The victory of Margaret Thatcher in 1979 was a watershed, and the era of free-market dominance is still with us, as we flex our Britannic muscles in the wake of the Referendum of 2016. For me, it is a sweep of history full of vivid memories, and at every stage I have been stimulated to reflect upon it all and learn what I could.

A long life has also conferred on me innumerable blessings, above all a rich, supportive family life and many long-term friendships and professional relationships. My debts are happily incalculable. I gladly acknowledge first the thorough scrutiny of the numerous drafts of this book by the Revd Canon Dr Malcolm Brown and the Revd Canon Peter Fisher, whose suggestions have been invaluable. I also warmly thank Professor Ann Loades for her comments and her deep encouragement, not only over this book but also through decades of friendship that began when we became colleagues in the Theology Department of Durham University. The whole staff welcomed me in 1979, and over twenty-two bracing years provided me with a congenial home for exploration. I was able to complete my doctorate on William Temple and convert it into a book for the wider public, and also venture to Germany, Japan and South Korea. I particularly treasure the collegiality and personal friendship of Professor Dr Oswald Bayer of the University of Tübingen, the Revd Shigeko Yamano of the Anglican Nippon Sei Ko Kai, Japan, and Dr Hyun-Ah Kim and the Revd Dr Deuk-Hoon Park from South Korea. And whilst I came to encounter many different traditions within the Christian faith, including Russian Orthodoxy in its cultural context, I also grew in appreciation of the diverse Anglican tradition. I deeply value what I learned from Professor Stephen Sykes and Professor Daniel Hardy, who put me in the best position to recognize the immense gifts of Dr Rowan Williams, Archbishop of Canterbury from 2002 to 2012. His depth of insight into the challenge of the gospel to the world and the Church itself has excited and sustained me for decades.

I wish warmly to thank the dear people of St Michael and All Angels, Witton Gilbert, for the community life they have provided over the last fifty-three years. It was in 2007–8 that we conducted a series of conversations over many months to ask fundamental questions about why we were there as church, and what shape we wished to see for our church life as we moved into an uncertain future. We saw the Eucharist as lying at the very centre of our lives, whilst wanting at the same time to connect much more fully with the life of the village and the wider world. It was in answer to our prayers that soon afterwards the Revd Canon Caroline Dick became priest-in-charge. She led us in a catholic worship which was both reverent and open to the world, and she was able to turn us outwards with her imaginative concept of Breathing Space—a project for the health and wellbeing of all, which was both collaborative with other agencies and also distinctive in its Christian basis. She had the invaluable gift of encouraging the laity to discover their diverse latent talents, so as to work together for the growth of our own church life and to implement the project through all the challenges of recent years. I warmly thank Caroline for all her inspiration and encouragement. Though the project finds only brief expression in this book in the Appendices, it is entirely complementary to its content, and has done much to convince me that theological reflection must be rooted in and flow out of a whole life lived daily and concretely in a faith centred on the Word made flesh.

Within the wider Church I wish to pay tribute to the late Revd Canon Bill Hall, Senior Arts and Recreation Chaplain in North-East England, and his colleagues the Revd Robert Cooper and the Revd Francis Minay, and to two Chairmen of the Board of Trustees, the late Ken Bates and the Revd Canon Professor David Jasper. I was on the Board as Secretary for over thirty years and deeply appreciated the way they promoted the arts and recreation at all levels of Church and society. It only ever seems to be a more imaginative minority in the life of the Anglican Church who appreciate the importance of the arts, and this experiment has very sadly long been in abeyance. I can only hope this book does much to revitalize recognition of the promise of the arts in the life of society and Church.

It was a real privilege to serve for fourteen years as Secretary to the Board of the company and charity Parents Against Child Exploitation (Pace) UK (formerly CROP). For me, it was a great learning experience about a scourge of our culture which reflects its deep malaise, and sadly the incidence of child sexual exploitation always far outstrips the capacity of the charity to support affected parents and protect children. I wish them well in their continuing determined struggles.

I wish also to record my grateful thanks for the long-term support and counsel of the Revd Canon Peter Kenney. I have been able to go and sit with him and talk through my experience of life in all its many changes, and to find a listening ear and a wise head and heart. It has been a priceless source of reassurance and strength.

Finally I gladly pay tribute to the high standards of journalism set and maintained by the *Guardian* and its staff. Their commitment to investigating and presenting the truth is second to none, and it is an absolute lifeline at a time when low-grade politics and journalism intersect in unprincipled and destructive ways.

All these experiences and many more have, I believe, put me in a position to address our present cultural predicament. I do this first on a humanistic basis, in a critical and constructive fashion, asking such questions as who we are as persons, what sort of a world we live in, what kinds of knowledge are open to us, and what is to count as rational. I then explore supporting forms of the Christian faith, with the overall aim of presenting a vision and stance of sufficient depth to sustain a flourishing common life together and provide a credible interweaving of worship, faith and action in the world.

In the production of this book, I wish to thank Church House Publishing for their kind permission to reproduce several paragraphs from my essay "The Temple Tradition" in Malcolm Brown (ed.), *Anglican Social Theology* (2014). I also thank the Cambridge Private Law Centre for permission to quote from Lord Sumption's Cambridge Freshfields Annual Law Lecture, "Government by decree—Covid-19 and the Constitution", given on 27 October 2020.

Introduction

Why I have written this book

Forty years ago, it had become common practice to divide sharply between the public and the private realms. The public realm was taken to be a rational place, one of objective fact, mechanical and deterministic, with technocratic manipulation of things and persons in the name of utility. By contrast, all other values were seen as purely subjective and relegated to the private realm, a position known as emotivism: values, whether artistic, moral or religious, are matters of individual feeling or taste, void of cognitive truth, and therefore irrational.

This division was the latest twist in the long Anglo-Saxon story of a sceptical search to determine what is to count as assured knowledge. In 1936, A. J. Ayer had published *Language, Truth and Logic*, which launched the era of logical positivism. This was actually Austrian in origin, but well attuned to the Anglo-Saxon mentality. Only mathematics and the various sciences could pass muster as publicly agreed knowledge and so count as meaningful; art, morality and religion were disqualified and confined to the private realm.

Ayer later admitted that with hindsight the fundamental criterion he had applied to secure this distinction (the so-called "verification principle") was not self-evident truth but only a "stipulative definition", which is just erudite language for "Let's suppose". Yet forms of logical positivism are still powerful. For it is really an episode in the insatiable human (well, mostly male) quest for the Holy Grail of knowledge which is cleansed of any emotion and truly impersonal. This would be satisfying to many not only intellectually but very practically. For if it were attainable, then everyone would have to accept it and live in terms of it.

Thus Friedrich von Hayek, taking a strongly liberal view of human freedom, thought he had found a secure, rational basis for free-market economics which would put an end for ever to the case for socialism of any hue. The market is taken to be an autonomous realm, entirely neutral over values and purposes. It is an arena that individuals and businesses are free to enter, each pursuing their self-chosen goals, and bound only by its procedural rules. Its outcomes are similarly value-neutral. The society in which the market is embedded has no purpose over and above the choices of its individual citizens. Hayek therefore considered any talk of social and economic justice to be intellectually and morally disreputable. It is rather surprising that his ideas were so slow to be taken up in capitalist countries, until he and Milton Friedman became the gurus of Margaret Thatcher and Ronald Reagan. For such notions are very attractive to the economically successful, seeming to give them the high intellectual and moral ground. No wonder the cry went up, "There is no alternative", as the weaker sections of the population were expected to accept their lot of permanent subservience within the vagaries of Hayek's economic universe.

Forty years ago, this twinning of technocracy and emotivism was thoroughly examined, but evidently with little effect. In his 1981 book *The Irony of Liberal Reason*, the American political philosopher Thomas A. Spragens, Jr saw it as one product of the ambivalent project known as the Enlightenment, originating in the seventeenth century. On the one hand, it had given us noble ideals: civil rights and liberties, representative institutions, the political role of reason and persuasion, limited government and respect for human dignity and equality. It had also promoted the amazing rise of modern science. On the other hand, the ironic flaw of liberalism was that it had not only been incapable of sustaining its humane goals but even threatened to undermine them. The West was now imperilled by an unstable interaction of technocracy and emotivism. For the technocrat and the emotivist share the basic conviction that the only assured knowledge is mathematical and scientific. But values persist in appearing in the public realm and laying claims upon us. The technocrat, if he sees them at all, blithely claims that they are justified by his science, whereas the emotivist insists that all values belong to the private realm, as matters merely of individual taste. So there is an oscillation back and forth between two dubious positions, often in the same individual. The net result is that the combination dangerously leaves moral claims groundless, and so leaves moral passions homeless.

In the same year, Alasdair MacIntyre produced *After Virtue: A Study in Moral Theory*, the first volume in his trilogy of books on the liberal project. He expressed disquiet that our public moral arguments are interminable, since there seems no way of securing moral agreement in the public realm. He exposed the mistakes and incoherences embedded in our technocratic-emotivist culture: in essence, the technocrat is focussed on means, which presuppose values and ends, but these cannot be rationally discussed, so that in the public arena power will be exercised arbitrarily.

These strictures have largely gone unheeded. Unsurprisingly, in the last forty years, the dyke between the public and private realms has broken down, and the public realm is now awash with emotion, often of passionate intensity. It has become all the easier to have one's cake and eat it: the technocrat can insist on his scientific certainty, but if others won't accept it, then he feels free aggressively to push through his own preferences.

Thus scientific and technocratic thinking are still pre-eminent, and Hayekian free-market economics still has its fervent devotees. As Naomi Klein shows, those who doggedly deny the climate change emergency still treat their own free-market assumptions as common sense and scientifically true, whilst seeing in their opponents a diabolical socialist plot.[1] Now that emotion engulfs the public realm, there is little pretence at rational argument in the marketplace of ideas, and free-marketeers no longer have any compunction in intensifying their pursuit of influence and power. Not content with the enormous capacity they have to lobby governments, in 2016, they managed in the USA to take the reins of political power, coupling hard economics with an emotive promise to "make America great again".

The rise of social media has been exploited to the full. The principal technique is the steady denigration of one's opponents by sowing doubt or spreading innuendo or presenting "alternative facts". A major target has been any section of the media which maintains that its journalistic task is to hold power to account in a rational and truthful manner. We have the ruthless determination, sometimes open but often underhand, to neutralize any possible countervailing institution and achieve an unassailable dominance. Of course, such behaviour is nothing new; it is found in the brazen *realpolitik* of the Athenians towards the Melians 2,500 years ago: "The strong do what they can, and the weak suffer what they must."[2] But it is now lamentably underwritten by technocracy-emotivism, which so pervades our mindset and permeates every facet of life that we scarcely notice it. That is a major part of our predicament, which leaves us wide open to exploitation.

In the UK, there is a similar combination of hard-nosed Hayekian free-market economics with a sentimental nostalgic nationalism. There are important questions about forms of economics and the place and role of the democratic nation-state in a global world, but these were not worked through at the time of the 2016 Referendum. Brexit unfortunately triggered a resurgence of English exceptionalism, the taking back of control after decades of being a "vassal" of the European Union, to resume being Britannia, a free independent global power. Our negotiations with the EU to secure an ever-harder Brexit were guided by immediate interest and advantage, with no compunction about backtracking on undertakings, as is clear over Ireland. It was about the accumulation and exercise of power, with contempt for any who might presume to check it.

There is growing evidence in the United Kingdom of a grave threat to Parliament, the judiciary, the civil service, the BBC, and to our very understanding of democracy. The government's proroguing of Parliament in 2019 was unanimously declared null and void by the Supreme Court, yet the Attorney General immediately told the House of Commons it was a dead Parliament. Heads of civil service departments have been removed and replaced by more pliant occupants. The BBC is endlessly threatened, whether with more financial penalization, with a hostile chairman, or because of alleged bias in reporting. The 2019 Conservative manifesto promised a commission "to restore trust in democracy". Yet the government's own conduct in recent years inspires no confidence in such a restoration, only the fear of further erosion.

Lady Hale has trenchantly criticized the way Parliament surrendered its role in scrutinizing the government's exercise of sweeping powers over the coronavirus emergency. In October 2020, Jonathan Sumption, a former Supreme Court judge, dissected the way the government, taking advantage of people's fears over the coronavirus, had arrogated emergency powers so as to minimize accountability to Parliament. "Governments hold power in Britain on the sufferance of the elected chamber of the legislature. Without that we are no democracy." He warned:

> The present government has a different approach. It seeks to derive its legitimacy directly from the people, bypassing their elected representatives ... It [has] revealed a cavalier disregard for the limits of [its] legal powers which has continued to characterise the government's behaviour ... Authoritarian rulers sustain themselves in power by appealing to the emotional and irrational in collective opinion ... The British public has not even begun to understand the seriousness of what is happening to our country.[3]

On 30 December 2020, MPs were allocated a risible five hours to debate a document 1246 pages long on the "deal" between the UK and the EU. The Leader of the House of Commons declared that this was merely the "icing on the Christmas cake that the Prime Minister delivered for the nation". So much for the reclaiming of parliamentary sovereignty! The Prime Minister announced the triumph of "cakeism": the restoration of full sovereignty while ensuring free access to European markets. This is simply untrue: there is the agreed Northern Ireland protocol, and there are many costly hurdles to trade to be negotiated by businesses.

It is clear that the new "deal" is a combination of two elements. First, there is a further entrenchment of Hayekian economics. Its libertarian dynamic is starkly incompatible with the simultaneous quasi-moral talk of "levelling up" within the UK. It therefore remains to be seen how far commitment to state investment will go, especially in the wake of the astronomical costs of COVID. It is likely to be dispensed in a limited fashion and to be targeted to consolidate and enhance Conservative power, in readiness for any general election. Meanwhile the revelations in the Pandora Papers about shell firms and tax havens for the super-rich, legally or illegally depleting tax revenues and undermining our democracy, will doubtless go unaddressed; for a "cash for access" culture aimed principally at the super-rich is shamelessly entrenched at the heart of our government.⁴ Secondly, there is full rein given to an emotive English nationalism which perpetuates an indulgent view of our imperial history. The common factor is "freedom from constraint". It is indeed "Britannia Unchained". This is apparently what Brexit meant all along. All this does nothing to heal our divisions; it is the very stuff of culture wars.

It must be said that "freedom from constraint", whilst an essential element in an account of freedom, is seriously inadequate on its own. It can easily translate into depriving others of their freedom, as we shall see in Part 1 in the case of the burgeoning slave trade. In a right-wing Hayekian context, it reflects rampant individualism, epitomized by the Prime Minister's declaration that from 19 July 2021 we would "move from universal government diktat to relying on people's personal responsibility". This is a false view of persons, who are at once individual and communal, and of government, which is there to serve our personal common life. We shall meet a much deeper understanding of freedom in Part 4: freedom to be fully human.

These profound problems cannot be properly addressed if we remain mired in technocracy-emotivism. They require a fresh approach. This will involve not the wholesale repudiation of liberalism or markets, but certainly the rejection of the initial premise of the technocrat and the emotivist alike: that the only assured knowledge is scientific or mathematical, and all else is irrational emotion.

Mark Carney, Governor of the Bank of England 2013–20, has trenchantly exposed the folly of compartmentalizing economics and stripping value from any relationship to its social and political context. Economists have come to assume that values are merely subjective preferences not open to reasoned argument, and that the act of pricing an activity or good does not alter its underlying nature. But that leads to market pricing being taken to represent intrinsic value; and if something is not in the market, it is not valued. The result is extreme commodification as commerce expands deep into the personal and civic realms. Quite simply, the price of everything becomes the value of everything. The financial crisis, the pandemic and the climate emergency all reflect twisted economics, amoral culture and institutions lacking accountability and integrity. Carney sets out at length seven key values:

solidarity, fairness, responsibility, resilience, sustainability, dynamism and humility, and argues that any good society requires fairness between the generations and in the distribution of income and life chances.[5] I am dealing with the same issues but approach them from a different angle.

It should be clear that with Hayek and other technocrats we are dealing not with fact or pure logic but with ideology. An ideology is both an intellectual posture and also a practical strategy. All ideologies have leading ideas which necessarily involve values and excite intense emotions, and all ideologues are prone to claim they have the key to terminate all argument. Marxism is an excellent illustration from the left wing: it claimed to be scientific; it derided morality as a by-product of bourgeois interests; yet it was driven by great moral fervour. This is no surprise, since capitalism and communism are horses from the same stable—the Enlightenment—and virtual mirror images. But, of course, ideologies are found the world over.

All ideologies make assumptions about the nature of human beings and the world we live in. In Hayek's case, the world can be neatly compartmentalized, so that the public realm is dominated by a purely autonomous economics. There is also a dualistic reading of the fundamental nature of human beings. They are free individuals in a mechanical universe, rational actors bound only by procedural rules in the economic sphere, whilst their bonds of solidarity with other human beings are never a given in life but always to be self-chosen.

In sum, all ideologies are inherently contentious. Often their plausibility is achieved by a process of cerebral abstraction. This is typical in the West, where, ever since Descartes, the mind has been treated as the essence of human beings, often in sharp distinction from the body, which has been viewed as the seat of the emotions and a mere mechanism for manipulation. This piece of dualism is a catastrophic misreading of persons, who are an indissoluble unity of many dimensions: spirit, soul, mind, body, emotions. I will explore the issue of dualism more fully in Part 2.

The acid test of an ideology is how it plays out in the ordinary concrete lives of actual human beings. We have to ask whether it does justice to the riches of personal life. I am reminded of Robert F. Kennedy's remarks when seeking the Democratic Party's presidential nomination in 1968: "The Gross National Product does not allow for the health of our children, the quality of their education or the joy of their play. It does not include the beauty of our poetry or the strength of our marriages... It measures... neither our wisdom nor our compassion... It measures everything, in short, except that which makes our life worthwhile."[6]

The initial concern of this book is therefore to recognize the dangers of technocracy-emotivism: that it combines a narrow technical rationality with irrationalism in a way which is inherently divisive and destructive of culture. As Robert and Edward Skidelsky have pointed out, civilizations have assumed that some ways of life are intrinsically superior to others. They have spoken of the good life, with its virtues and ends, and seen them as crucial for our ability to find meaning in our human lives. St Augustine remarked that all human perversity comes from the confusion of means and ends. But modern economics has dispensed with these assumptions. It is true that a liberal society permits any number of visions of the good life, but it is by the same token hospitable to none of them. For it forbids any *public* preference for this or that way of life. It is a testimony to its acute individualism. By contrast, we are a social species, so the good life is essentially a life in common with others. Its home is in groups of people doing things together—not in the brains of individuals.[7] The question is: Can we chart such a society and culture? We must try, and I believe we can.

The structure of this book

Alasdair MacIntyre has a very different reading from modern liberal economics, fundamentally over the nature of knowledge and persons. "I am my body and my body is social, born to those parents in this community with a specific social identity."[8] He thus starts out from our concrete historical living in society, with natural bonds of solidarity, familial and civil, and a wealth of associations within which we can flourish. Though fact and value need to be distinguished in thought, in human life they are inseparably bound up together. This leads MacIntyre to the idea of a practice. Typical examples are the numerous professions, the enquiries of the sciences, the work of the historian, the artist, the musician, indeed the whole endeavour of creating and sustaining the culture of human communities. These are all co-operative activities, coherent and socially established; they cultivate the virtues necessary to pursue their proper standards of excellence and so realize the public goods internal to them. They are never a matter of preference or taste, or of purely technical skills, for they can be rationally discussed in the pursuit of the goods and ends inherent in the practice.

I shall be taking my cue from MacIntyre as I set out on the quest for a basis for our culture which is capable of healing the divisions in our country. I claim that it is a mistake to privilege mathematical and scientific knowledge, as if they gave us the decisive key to knowledge and building a culture. There are many different human practices which have their own inherent logic and rationality, and all have their place in a well-rounded human culture. I draw on many authors in the last hundred years to show the broad support for such a view of knowledge. Thus I reject the pursuit of the Holy Grail of impersonal knowledge, and I shall agree with Michael Polanyi that it is actually a contradiction in terms. All knowledge is personal knowledge, embracing both objective and subjective dimensions. Knowledge is indeed of what is out there, and we do grasp the nature of the universe. But there is a personal commitment made in every form of knowing. This is because of our very nature as persons. Whatever our intellectual attainments, we are always rooted in our physical and emotional life, and we are most likely to find personal knowledge if we stay with the ordinary concrete world of space and time which we all inhabit and experience. Thus the experience of any and every human being is of importance and should be taken into account in the unending public deliberation on what is due to us as diverse members of the human race. The tendency to bow to technical experts is a sign of our flight from the human quest for the good life. We need to recover the confidence that this is a matter of recognizing our common humanity, at once individual and social, and living it out in a common life, where we constantly share and reflect on our diverse experiences.

In Part 1, I draw on many writers to build up a conspectus of various forms of knowledge, each with their practical role to play in the common enterprise of human culture. I deliberately confine myself at this stage to humanistic writing, that is, writing reflecting on our common experience of personal living, without explicit reference to any religious position.

This choice needs a little explanation. It is unusual for Christians, who tend to begin with the Bible as the revealed Word of God and often take a negative view of the world. However, direct appeal to revelation is by no means unproblematic, both because we live a common life in a plural society, and because historically Christianity has itself been understood in diverse ways, and in the West, it has been prone to deep internal conflicts and heavy-handed external action in society. Moreover, Christians have often tended to assume that the faith is addressed directly to individuals, to convert them and save their souls, and only indirectly, if at all, to societies and cultures. This has been productive of numerous dualisms, such as individual/society, inner/outer, spirit/matter, faith/culture. By contrast, Christians need to develop more confidence that they can enter into reasoned discussion with their fellow-citizens on matters of public concern, without setting aside their faith. Reasoned discourse is part and parcel of living the Christian life, like any other, and truth is to be recognized wherever it is found.

The question arises concerning which forms of Christian faith are best able to support and sustain the humanitarian position adopted in Part 1. Because of the diversity and the dualisms, Part 2 involves a great deal of clearing of the ground. To do this I have chosen to enter into conversation with Jeremy Lent. In *The Patterning Instinct: A Cultural History of Humanity's Search for Meaning*, he has fascinatingly surveyed numerous cultures and the root metaphors they have used to construct meaning in their world. He sees a looming struggle between two contrasting views of humanity. One is driving us to a technological endgame of artificially enhanced humans. The other enables a sustainable future arising from our intrinsic connectedness with each other and the natural world. He is primarily attracted to Chinese ways of approaching the question of meaning in our lives. He gives an account of Christianity as manifestly a major part of our cultural predicament, and in no way offering a solution. So the conversation centres on the nature and role of Christianity in Western culture.

This is a further fundamental reason for writing this book. Lent speaks trenchantly of a cascade of dualism flowing from Plato, where there is a cosmological dualism which runs right through every person in the form of a body–soul dualism. This was to structure the European tradition of thought about humanity and the universe all the way to the present. There is much truth in this account. Lent believes that the dualism intensified in Western Christianity in large part due to St Paul and St Augustine, and was perpetuated by Descartes and the whole Enlightenment project. I accept that he gives us copious evidence of this dualism in Western Christianity. But I submit that he is tendentious and in places inaccurate, and I set out a different interpretation of the Christian faith.

I hold that Christianity is not in essence a dualistic religion, but a religion of unity-in-diversity. In distinction from Platonism, Christianity is a religion which is thoroughly personal and relational. God is Trinitarian, the ultimate unity-in-diversity, freely creating the world, and choosing to be the God of what is not God. Nor is there any dualism of the person: far from putting spirit and matter in opposition, Christianity starts out from the unity of the person, within which are diverse capacities: spirit, soul, mind, body, emotions. It holds us to the sheer God-given physicality of ourselves and our world. Sin is not a sign of inherent dualism, but a rupture in relationships which God, through fidelity to the covenant, originally with the people of Israel, has constantly sought to restore; this culminated in God's decisive act in Jesus Christ to reconcile all things into a final unity-in-diversity.

What sort of view of God would endorse and underpin the understanding of culture portrayed in Part 1? I propose that if the whole cultural process is a deeply personal movement, then we need a source who is no less than personal, to be both generative of the whole process and at all times intimately involved in fostering its growth.

There are at least two strands in the Anglican tradition which would be supportive of this approach. The first strand is the dialogic approach of William Temple and his successors, which I set out in *Anglican Social Theology* (2014), edited by Malcolm Brown, in the chapter "The Temple Tradition". The other is the integralist approach, in origin Roman Catholic, sketched by the late John Hughes in the same volume in "After Temple? The Recent Renewal of Anglican Social Thought". I therefore offer in Part 2 a first statement of an integralist understanding of the relation of faith and culture. It rejects the dualistic supposition of two tiers, a natural and a supernatural, and seeks a more integral schema. The fundamental idea is that nature never exists in abstraction from God but is created and sustained by God's grace. This does not equate to dogmatic dictation to the world, or a refusal to engage with it. On the contrary, the Christian must enter into open dialogue with the world we all inhabit in common. Indeed the point of an integralist approach is precisely for a more thorough engagement with the contemporary world. Readers can work out for themselves where they wish to stand on the issues raised, and how far they are persuaded by the course of the discussion.

Parts 3 and 4 therefore set out much more fully this understanding of Christianity, first of its principal act of worship, and then of the faith.

Part 3 is devoted to the Liturgy. Liturgy is so often taken to be arcane and archaic, an area for those given to private religiosity. Actually, the term "liturgy" is straight out of the ordinary world. In the ancient world, citizens competed with each other to bring glory to their city state and were prepared to say thank you to the gods by financing some great work. It might be a temple, or perhaps a warship to keep your city on top of its rivals. Of course it also brought honour to you and your family. You gladly performed your *leitourgia*, a word composed of *laos* (people) and *ergon* (work). So it is simply "the work of the people", and in those days it would always have a religious character.

The Liturgy is best thought of as a drama in several acts. It is a thanksgiving (*eucharistia*), a concentrated acting out of the Christian story of what God has done in creation, particularly for the human race, and focally through the life, death and resurrection of Jesus Christ and the re-creation of a community, now known as the Church. Its members gather, bringing with them their ordinary life in the world, and enter into the movement of that drama, in order to become more and more truly what by baptism they already are, the body of Christ, and to invite the world to see its own true life and destiny in that movement.

Our chief guide will be Gregory Dix through his monumental work, *The Shape of the Liturgy*. Born George Dix in London in 1901, he became a novice in an Anglican Benedictine order and took the name Gregory. He spent most of his adult life at Nashdom Abbey in Buckinghamshire and published the book in 1945. His concern was to study the history of the Liturgy intensively in order to form a clear idea of what shape and content was absolutely at the core. He was not a scholar's scholar, a kind of liturgical archaeologist or antiquarian, but deeply concerned with the lives of ordinary people. He believed that worship was the giving of glory to God, and that we owed it as human beings to get it as right as we could. But also, if Christianity is about the creation and redemption of the world by God, then we also need to get it right for the world's sake. Worship is a form of witness to the world. He believed that the *Book of Common Prayer* had serious deficiencies and was distressed when Parliament turned down the attempt at its revision in 1928. Indeed, it seemed to him plain wrong that Parliament had the power to lock the Church of England into the Elizabethan settlement for evermore. The results of his researches, along with many other scholars and practitioners across the churches, fed into widespread liturgical reforms, including *Common Worship*.

Gregory Dix wanted to recover the finest Liturgy. His concern for the world comes out most fully on the very last page of *The Shape of the Liturgy*, where in the midst of the Second World War he wrote:

> "There is one human race in which the mysteries of God are fulfilled." [St Irenaeus] ... The dream of the self-sufficiency of human power has haunted the hearts of all men since it was first whispered that by slipping from under the trammels of the law of God "Ye shall be as Gods", choosing your own good and evil ... In its crudest form, in the politics of our day, the pagan dream of human power has turned once more into a nightmare oppressing men's outward lives. That will pass, because it is too violent a disorder to be endured. But elsewhere and less vulgarly, as a mystique of technical and scientific mastery of man's environment, it is swiftly replacing the old materialism as the prevalent anti-christianity of the twentieth century. In this subtler form it will more secretly but even more terribly oppress the human spirit.

This clearly has a strong resonance with Part 1, which has in view particularly the question of our common humanity and the loss, defence and primacy of persons.

Dix's work came out seventy-five years ago, and it has been contested at various points. He was prone to overplay his hand over the historical evidence for his position and was too schematic. I have relied on Paul F. Bradshaw and Maxwell E. Johnson, *The Eucharistic Liturgies: Their Evolution and Interpretation* (2012) to keep abreast of the latest developments. I am also aware that Dix's life was centred very much in the Anglo-Catholic world in which he grew up, and he did not have much empathy for Protestantism. He wrestled long and hard over whether he should join the Church of Rome and resolved in the end to be an Anglican Papalist, working towards the reunion of the Anglican Church with Rome. None the less I believe that his interpretation of the shape and understanding of the Liturgy that was prevalent by the fifth century is basically correct and has rightly informed modern Eucharistic revision; it is therefore vital for the life of the Church and the world. Moreover, though he died in 1952, ten years before the Second Vatican Council, at which integralist thinking first made its impact, he is in tune with it, particularly in his grasp of the relation of the Eucharist to the once-for-all sacrifice of Christ himself. I have also taken account of Simon Bailey, *A Tactful God: Gregory Dix, Priest, Monk and Scholar* (1995), and Simon Jones (ed.), *The Sacramental Life: Gregory Dix and His Writings* (2007).

Many years ago, I read A. E. Welsford's *Life in the Early Church A.D. 33–313*, published in 1951. She was a born teacher, with a real gift for storytelling. I have drawn on her lively reconstructions of life in the ancient world.

Gregory Dix focussed on the Liturgy of the Eucharist with its distinctive shape and content. Part 4 sets out the fuller content of the Christian faith through study of Rowan Williams, who was for ten years Archbishop of Canterbury. He has consistently engaged in critical and constructive dialogue with the contemporary world and worked both ecumenically and in conversation with people of other religious faiths and none. He has practised a dialogic and integralist theology. In the secular world, he has been denigrated by those who think he has trespassed on their turf, but he has won respect for his openness to interdisciplinary dialogue, and many have acknowledged his acute perceptiveness about life from a Christian perspective. Within the Anglican Communion he has been widely appreciated for his wisdom; but others have proved incapable of grasping his deep roots in the faith and have rejected his stance. I have drawn on many of his works, particularly *On Christian Theology*. Above all, his *Christ the Heart of Creation* is his fullest interpretation of the Christian faith. It is the culmination of decades of intensive ecumenical study and discussion, Orthodox, Catholic and Protestant, ranging from seventh-century St Maximus the Confessor to twentieth-century Dietrich Bonhoeffer. It is the finest exposition I know of the foundations of the Christian faith and how it can inform the Church's approach to the contemporary world. I have tried to make it as accessible as possible to a wider public.

Parts 3 and 4 are thus very dependent for their substance on Gregory Dix and Rowan Williams, but they are expressed in my own way to fit with the purpose of this work. I have included two Appendices to show a dialogic and integralist approach in action.

I have written as an Anglican and need to say something about the ethos of Anglicanism. It has many strands, which do not neatly dovetail into one another. That is nothing new. Anglicans have often said that they are more likely to get nearer the truth if they listen to others within the Anglican Communion and beyond it, rather than ignore or oppose one another. Behind that lies a Christian history of bruising encounters, unedifying battles, and even appalling atrocities. Today we say we believe in resolving differences by open dialogue. But the subject inevitably arouses great passions, and if some unfamiliar position comes to our ears, there can be bewilderment and a defensiveness which can rapidly become outright rejection. The interpretation of Christianity I present here differs from that held by many. I have made a statement of Christianity and its implications from within one part of the spectrum of Anglicanism, whilst attending to the rest. I am also well aware that any strand needs to be constantly on the move, trying to discern the most faithful way of inhabiting the Christian faith.

This work is not primarily academic but is offered to anyone who cares sufficiently about our culture to invest the necessary time and effort to discern the way forward out of our predicament towards a more healthy and flourishing culture on firmer foundations. I am asking: is there here, in this approach, a vision and stance of sufficient depth that it can address our cultural predicament and inspire further exploration for the sake of our common cultural life and a credible interweaving of worship, faith and action in the world?

I have had my say, and it is for others to pursue that exploration along a journey which is always necessarily incomplete. Like William Temple, I remain the proverbial "Jones", asking what there is to eat.[9]

Notes

[1] Naomi Klein, *On Fire: The Burning Case for a Green New Deal*, pp. 70f.
[2] Thucydides, *The History of the Peloponnesian War*, Book V. 89.
[3] Jonathan Sumption, "Government by decree—Covid-19 and the Constitution", *Cambridge Freshfields Annual Law Lecture*, delivered 27 October 2020 at the Cambridge Private Law Centre.
[4] Rowena Mason, Luke Harding, Harry Davies, "The Tory Donor King", *The Guardian*, 6 October 2021, p. 11.
[5] Mark Carney, *Value(s): Building a Better World for All*, esp. pp. 124–46.
[6] Quoted in Michael J. Sandel, *Justice: What's the Right Thing to Do?*, pp. 262f. Original at <https://www.jfklibrary.org/learn/about-jfk/the-kennedy-family/robert-f-kennedy/robert-f-kennedy-speeches/remarks-at-the-university-of-kansas-march-18-1968>, accessed 28 December 2021.
[7] Robert and Edward Skidelsky, *How Much is Enough? Money and the Good Life*, pp. 86–95.
[8] Alasdair MacIntyre, *After Virtue: A Study in Moral Theory*, p. 172.
[9] F. A. Iremonger, *William Temple, Archbishop of Canterbury: His Life and Letters*, p. 162.

PART 1

Our Culture

Along with many other areas of the world Britain faces a challenge which is daunting in its scale and complexity. On so many fronts it is divided. Its divisions seem continually to multiply and morph, and to cut across one another. Confrontations are actively fomented, and disagreements rapidly become polarized. Language is often vacuous or venomous. There is growing suspicion and a steep decline in trust. The way through to a country at peace with itself seems ever more opaque and elusive.

This challenge is surely first and foremost cultural. But this must not be a warrant for a further surge in culture wars. It requires us to investigate all the areas of life which contribute to our culture: to attend closely to our lived experience, to see how we came to reach this impasse, and to unearth the assumptions which we often unwittingly carry deep within us. This is not a task we can hand over to government or technicians or any other group: it calls for all to play the role for which they are best suited.

So can Humpty be put together again? I suspect "again" is a misnomer, since the first step may well be to set aside the fond delusion that there ever was a Golden Age to be restored. But we certainly do need to avail ourselves of whatever resources are already at hand to help us on our way. This Part 1 is therefore not only analytical but also constructive, drawing on much humanistic material.

Who are the "we" and "our"? My immediate focus is Britain, particularly England, but the issues are pretty common across the Western world, and indeed anywhere affected by its global reach. I now review our cultural life, starting with the area which has been so dominant in recent decades.

Economics, politics and society

In 1945, flush with triumph in war, Britain was expected to vote in Winston Churchill to "finish the job" and "win the peace". There was much international consternation when it was Clement Attlee who swept to power with a landslide victory. Clearly the majority in the country were looking for a new start and, after all the trauma and sacrifice of war, were not prepared to be dragged back to the 1930s, with their economic depression, mass unemployment, multiple poverty, and loss of self-esteem and human dignity, which the Jarrow March of 1936 had fruitlessly highlighted. Attlee was elected to inaugurate an extended welfare society, with a greatly enhanced peacetime role for the state. So came the creation of the NHS and widespread nationalization of basic industries.

This settlement endured until the 1970s, when we experienced stagflation, strife between government and trade unions, and the hikes in oil prices. In 1976, the Labour government had to approach the IMF for a loan and was obliged to devalue the pound. It seemed unable to deal with the pressures, and finally ran out of vitality. Margaret Thatcher had become leader of the Conservative Party in 1975. Her growing band of supporters passionately believed that the country had grown morally feeble on socialist welfare policies, and that we were now the laughingstock of Europe and the world for our incompetence and loss of virility.

In 1979, Mrs Thatcher came to power and inaugurated a new and increasingly coherent political experiment: at its core was capitalist free-market economics, backed by a strong but limited state, and a rugged individualism. So began an era of market triumphalism. Quoting St Francis of Assisi, she aimed to heal division and create a new and unassailable consensus.

Ever since 1979, the country has been divided over this project. Many welcomed the bracing entrepreneurial spirit and throve financially. At a stroke, the top rate of income tax was drastically cut, so that the better off could keep far more of their earnings, not only to improve the living standards of their families, but to invest in the economy and unleash its potential. The United Kingdom was to play a full-blooded role in the development of a global economy, and waves of deregulation expanded the opportunities for economic and financial success. The City of London increasingly became a powerful centre in world finance. Enthusiasm reached new heights when in 1982 President Galtieri took advantage of a lapse in British vigilance and made good Argentina's claim to the Falkland Islands, only to be trounced by Mrs Thatcher's audacious military response.

The Labour government under Tony Blair (1997–2007) endorsed much of her free-market approach as a means of financing its ambitious social policies. As the economy prospered, it set up initiatives like Sure Start for children in their early years and built many hospitals and schools through a combination of private and public finance. Under Gordon Brown, this strategy was radically undermined by the financial crash of 2008. This was not caused by some external force like a pandemic, but by its own internal dynamic, which had rested on the assumption that, whatever its excesses, the market would automatically self-correct to restore equilibrium. However, many people continued to put their faith in capitalism's powers of survival and self-transformation and prioritized restoring economic growth through global competition.

In 2010, the Conservatives returned to power in a coalition, scapegoated Labour for causing the whole problem by reckless profligacy, and pursued austerity for the next ten years. The Brexit issue cut across the usual right-left divide, and thanks primarily to dogged and dodgy campaigning by the relatively small core of Brexit devotees within the Conservative Party, the country voted in the 2016 Referendum by a narrow but decisive majority to free the country from the shackles of the European Union, "take back control", and pursue through its own global trade deals the restoration of Britain's prosperity and prestige.

Throughout this time, however, many had dissented strongly from "Thatcherism" and the lure of TINA ("there is no alternative"). Their lived experience of her policies was negative. They felt keenly the indifference to the rise of poverty, inequality and unemployment, even its welcome as "a price worth paying" for a bracing, competitive ethos (I well recall a government advertisement favouring the slimming down of the workforce in the steel industry: a man doing physical exercises to shed flab). There was the removal or reduction of many forms of social support and finally the imposition of the community charge ("poll tax"). Under the watchword "Managers are there to manage", there was the sidelining of the unions and the growing pressure to accept low-wage and low-quality jobs in a competitive market.

Mrs Thatcher famously said that there is no such thing as society; there are only individuals and their families.[1] This was part of her campaign to kill off socialism and give the primacy to individual resilience and resourcefulness. In the contrary experience of many, life was a struggle for the retention of any quality or dignity. It seemed to be a race to the bottom. The films of Ken Loach, such as *Sorry we missed you* and *I, Daniel Blake*, dramatically portray not only the ethos and practices of the system but also the inevitable relentless impact upon individual and family life. People resisted the slur that they were skivers over against the strivers, and the architects of their own misfortunes through their fecklessness. They deeply resented being told "Get on yer bike" to search for non-existent jobs, or to accept any job regardless of the humiliation involved. Whereas the government's definition of a "real job" was one in the private and not the state sector, for very many the cry "Gizza job" was one for quality and durability.

One predictable consequence of free-market policies was consumerism and high levels of personal debt. The commercial world readily provided not only a cornucopia of goods to satisfy perceived needs but a burgeoning stream of "must-have" novelties to stimulate further wants. As social psychologists have taught us, this is inseparable from the pursuit of status in society: we aspire to catch up with those higher up the scale and fear sinking to the status of those below. Richard Wilkinson and Kate Pickett in *The Spirit Level* document how in an already very unequal society we have become even more locked into a competitive struggle, and on every index inequality increases. There is a continuing decline in trust, and in the notion of a shared life in society.

Thatcherism remains a powerful force, if anything even more entrenched. It is important to see that it is in essence a form of economic ideology, and to grasp its main contours. Two thinkers came to be Mrs Thatcher's gurus: the American Milton Friedman and the Austrian Friedrich von Hayek. Both were Cold War warriors, convinced that any form of socialism, however mild, would slide into a totalitarian form.

For them, the market is an autonomous realm, and entirely neutral over values and purposes. It is an arena that individuals and businesses are free to enter, each pursuing their self-chosen goals, and bound only by its procedural rules. Its outcomes are similarly value-neutral; that is, simply factually what they are. Talk of justice over the market is as irrelevant as it is over the weather. Governments should therefore cease to interfere with the free operation of the market and concentrate on their proper job of defending the country from its enemies, external or internal, and ensuring citizens can go about their lawful business.

This view of the market was part of a wider philosophy. Friedman saw capitalism, freedom and democracy as parts of the same indivisible project. He advocated deregulation, privatization and cutbacks in social funding, in the belief that a truly free market created maximum benefits for all. Hayek extended his ideas on the market by arguing that Western society had left behind earlier restrictive forms and reached its ultimate form, the "Great Society", which had no purpose over and above the choices of its individual citizens. His strongly liberal view of justice and the rule of law led him to reject the notion of social and economic justice as a destructive mirage.[2]

In spite of the claim to neutrality over values, primacy is given here to ensuring maximal *economic* benefits in the form of the lowest prices in the long run, and also to the maximal freedom of the individual from constraint. These are clearly value choices, with predictable consequences. For they give pole position to the interests of risk-taking holders of wealth and discount the inherently social nature of human beings and their capacity to deliberate on a wide range of value-laden issues which are germane to pursuing the common good. The choices are inescapably political.

Even so, at the heart of recent government policy, whether "right" or "left", have been the autonomy of free-market economics, maximal growth and the satisfaction of individual consumer preferences. Under the assumption that "private ownership is good, public bad" huge swathes of the public sector have been privatized. Politicians have been nervous about interfering in the economic process; they have confined themselves largely to mimicking the market by monitoring economic performance, and making the necessary calculations to correct for market failure and ensure maximal effectiveness. They have shied off promoting values in public, preferring to stick with facts and quantifying. Yet, as Michael Sandel pointed out in the BBC Reith Lectures for 2009, *A New Citizenship*, there has long been an alternative view of politics. It has been about something more profound than this, namely the safeguarding and enhancing of the common good: promoting the health of democratic institutions and cultivating the solidarity and sense of community that democracy requires. And maximizing consumer satisfaction does nothing to make us democratic citizens.[3] Obsession with markets and money has ousted this alternative understanding of politics.

However, in another sense there is a marked continuity with the past. Thomas Piketty's monumental study *Capital and Ideology* (a sequel to his *Capital in the Twenty-First Century*) investigates on a world-wide scale how regimes have dealt with inequality. They have always had to do so, not so much because it has troubled their consciences, as because it threatened their dominance. Ever since the end of the Middle Ages, we have had ownership societies, based on the sanctity of private property and wealth. The ruling class has always had to struggle with how to reconcile the rest of society to this ideology. Piketty observes that they have repeatedly used the "slippery slope" notion to reject even the least concession, lest it lead inexorably to the collapse of their rule. There have been varying degrees of inequality across the centuries. The post-war period from 1945 to 1979 was something of a rarity: inequality was substantially reduced. The Thatcher years were thus really a counter-coup, a reassertion of the ownership type.

Science and technology

Whenever a country has expansive ambitions there has always been a close nexus between economic activity and the development of science and technology. It has been well said that our power internationally has depended on our technical inventiveness, from the longbow at Agincourt in 1415, through our shipbuilding prowess and navigation skills, to James Watt's invention of the steam engine. Peter Frankopan has written a history of the world from the geographical perspective of the Silk Roads across Asia. He documents the peculiar aggressiveness of the Western powers. British global expansion is typically Western; we distinguished ourselves by keeping ahead of the pack.[4]

So it was natural that capitalist free-market economics under Mrs Thatcher courted science and technology. This was partly to defend the country from envious enemies, partly to enhance competitiveness in the search for global leadership. In education, the sciences have been privileged and have great prestige in our society. The discipline of economics has itself been treated as a science, and one effect of this, and of the dominance of scientific and mathematical thinking more generally in the public realm, is the prevalence of models, measurements and statistics. Technical rationality comes to dominate. And since this readily leads to the prestige of technical experts, the ordinary citizen tends to be ruled by managerialism.

Closely related is a very utilitarian approach to decision-making, which involves making precise calculations to guide economic processes. This is a purely instrumental way of thinking. That is, it is entirely about means, and tends to bypass the matter of values or ends—which in turn makes economic values themselves, such as efficiency or cheapness, into ends. This is highly questionable. Certainly ethics has never been considered to be simply utilitarian calculus. It has always included a concern for character and the virtues, and for relationships and actions which are to be pursued and enjoyed as good in themselves. A major reason for the frenetic pace of modern life may well be our fearful and joyless obsession with utility and control without any adequate sense of the ends of life. The old belief that some ways of life are intrinsically superior to others has been swallowed in the insatiability we call growth and the endless expansion of wants in consumerism. Economics used to be a means to the good life, but the distinction between means and ends has now been obliterated.

The environment

These issues are evident in the matter of the environment. There has long been huge public concern both over increasing resource scarcity, and over the capacity of the planet to assimilate the environmental impact of our economic activity. IPCC reports have given no room for doubt about the global climate emergency, and that human activity is a major factor. Yet the history of policy in response has been disconcerting. The targets to which the advanced economies committed themselves have been missed by an alarming margin. It is worth noting gambits used hitherto which are increasingly seen to be deeply flawed.

"It's just maths." In the bitter haggling at the Copenhagen conference in 2009, the US climate change special envoy said that emissions were not about morality or politics, just about mathematics. The developed countries converted climate change issues into the cost-benefit game of carbon offsets and trading. Yet this offered no guarantee that emissions would fall, let alone keep the world within a 1.5 °C rise over preindustrial levels. Moreover, it ignored the plea of the global South that the North recognize its ecological debt to the South as a matter of justice.

"It's just economics." Attempts have been made to focus purely on the economic costs of climate change and of the policies needed to correct it. Yet it is clear that there is no easy compatibility of any adjusted economic activity and climate change. We need more than economic recalculation, rather a deeper enquiry into the causes of that change.

"It's just technical." No, technical fixes are never going to be sufficient, and are rarely neutral: they are so often undertaken to someone else's detriment.

"It's just science." It is widely assumed that environmental issues are basically scientific. Certainly scientific knowledge is essential. However, there are still questions about the nature of science (is it just the accumulating of facts?), and what else is crucial for the interpretation of climate change. The very ferocity of the battles between those who affirm and those who deny the climate emergency is evidence that they are not just about the accuracy of the science. At least in the Anglo-Saxon world, the deniers have been affronted over the threat to their practice of free-market economics. Moreover, they recognize a deep challenge to their nationalism, since climate change, like a pandemic, is no respecter of national boundaries.

COP26 left the strict limit of 1.5 °C "on life support", and the window of opportunity to save it is shrinking fast. It is clear that we desperately need to speed up a whole range of transitions. I do not simply mean those over fossil fuels, deforestation, soil, waste, fresh water and the oceans. We also need transitions over our assumptions or mindset about the kind of world we live in and who we are as persons. For the acceptance of the autonomy of economics, the obsession with endless growth and the satisfaction of individual consumer preferences are starkly incompatible with our finite ecological system. So here is a further range of necessary transitions:

We have to ditch the idea that we are free, rational individuals in a mechanical universe, which is there for us to manipulate, exploit and control as suits us. Nature actually consists of complex self-reinforcing systems which can patently be radically destabilized, but also have remarkable powers of self-regeneration. Our task is therefore to deepen our understanding of those systems and our place within them, and respectfully to work with their grain.

Instead of being obsessed with markets and money—"Leave it to the market"—we must abandon the belief that economics is an autonomous realm impervious to its social context of values, purposes and persons. Nationally we must stop treating politics merely as the handmaid of economics. Internationally the West's colonial pillaging and its heedlessness over its impact on the environment inescapably raise issues of social and economic justice.

Instead of us believing we are locked in a perpetual competitive struggle with all others for scarce resources, we need to uphold the conviction that we are primarily collaborative creatures in the task of developing our common life.

We must wean ourselves off emotivism. It encourages the delusion that we are individuals entitled to the first feeling or thought that occurs to us, passive consumers entitled to the satisfaction of our immediate wants. The incessant demand to "feel good" fixates us in triviality. Our horizons shrink, so we are wide open to the "greenwash" deceptions of producers and the blandishments of plausible politicians, the profit-seeking press and clever advertisers. We must recover the conviction that we are active citizens of a democratic parliamentary system, where we all share in sustained, rational deliberation in the pursuit of truth and the good life or common good.

Instead of prioritizing a narrow technical rationality, we need to recognize the whole range of human practices which go into the building of a rich culture. True, there is a place for calculating utility, but crucially there are also virtues and goods, ends as well as means.

We must also scotch the idea that we are primarily minds which theorize to solve problems. We humans are actually concrete beings of many dimensions, who need inner integration and a right relation with our social and natural environment. Each of us bears a dignity which calls for respect. The voices of those who suffer most should be given the prime attention. Above all, we need fresh, incisive insight and vigour from the younger generation.

Such transitions would surely mean a new relationship between central government, local and regional authorities, and movements and associations which spring up to further the common good. The notion of mutual assistance between different levels of society, where decisions are taken at the lowest feasible level (called "subsidiarity"), is nothing new—it is deeply embedded in the political tradition. Another consequence would undoubtedly be the curbing of the excesses of the rich and super-rich, including the closure of tax havens and a tax on wealth.

Above all, the narrative or story which has had us in thrall for at least the last forty years needs to be replaced by a new narrative or story which will carry conviction to the minds and hearts of ordinary people, and energize them for thorough engagement with the challenging quest for a flourishing culture and planet. I trust the following pages will aid that quest.

The Enlightenment: critique and response

The eminent economic historian R. H. Tawney used to say that in order to understand where we are, we may well need to go a long way upstream to find its source. So far we have been reviewing the last forty years. We now need to look back 400 years, to the rise of the movement known as the Enlightenment.

Thomas A. Spragens

In *The Irony of Liberal Reason* (1981), Thomas A. Spragens, Jr, an American political philosopher, describes his double sense of ambivalence and disquiet about the modern world. On the one hand, from the seventeenth century, we have the development of modern liberalism. It has been a progressive force. "Any humane political order ... must take with great seriousness the major concerns and ideals of this tradition: civil rights and liberties, representative institutions, the political role of reason and persuasion, limited government, respect for human dignity and equality." Yet many liberal ideas, attitudes and programmes seem disquietingly at odds with this humaneness. On the other hand, we have the rise of modern science, surely one of the most amazing achievements of human understanding. Yet Spragens is disturbed by narrow and misleading ideas of scientific rationality, which in turn are destructive of human culture.[5]

Spragens' thesis is that ironically "the same liberal tradition that is heir to and protector of Western humanism has developed within itself tendencies that threaten humane values". He observes that liberalism and scientific rationalism were twin-born, resting on the same philosophical basis. He investigates the course of this tradition, commonly known as the Enlightenment project.[6] We should accept the positive aspects, whilst engaging with the disquieting developments.

The new science of the seventeenth century challenged the Church principally on intellectual grounds, and in default of any careful relating of science and theology, gradually came to oust not only traditional theology but also the Greek philosophical legacy from Plato and Aristotle. Gone was a world permeated by forms and images and by *logos* (reason) in which we humans participated, and which ultimately ran into mystery. The emphasis moved instead to clear and simple ideas associated with physical things and sense data, and to mathematical axioms. The assumption was that the universe was not so much a mysterious whole as a mechanical assemblage.[7]

This was never just an academic matter. The end of knowledge was power. Descartes (1596–1650) hoped that the new knowledge would make humans "masters and possessors of nature". And this came to include human nature itself. For humans were assumed to be minds in machines. Indeed, for some thinkers all the operations of the mind were thought to be reducible to sensation. Enter the technocrat and the social engineer. They know the truth, and are called to manage those who are ignorant, for the good of society and their own good. Virtue was thus no longer embodied in a noble character; it was the practice of actions useful to the greatest number. Happiness was no longer a state of blessedness; it was reducible to pleasure, where all values became mere matters of taste.[8]

This all too brief sketch exposes the deep fracture in modern Western societies. The public realm has come to be seen as a rational place, one of objective fact, mechanical and deterministic, with technocratic manipulation of things and persons in the name of utility. Other values are purely subjective and are relegated to the private realm. This position is known as emotivism: values, whether moral, artistic or religious, are matters of individual feeling or taste, void of cognitive truth and irrational. They are simply lifestyle choices by individuals. Thomas Spragens' conclusion is that our culture is deeply threatened by the combination of technical rationality and emotivism, which feed off and so reinforce one another. It is an unstable pair, in that when values insist on cropping up in the public realm, the technocrat blithely treats the ones he likes as scientific fact, whereas the strict emotivist returns them all to the private realm. This is destructive of any vibrant culture.[9]

In response, Spragens' watchwords are "recognize", "exorcize" and "reconstruct". We have to recognize the roots of our predicament and break the spell of the "demons" that have us in thrall. To reconstruct, we have to address fundamental questions: What is involved in knowing? What kind of a world do we live in? And who are we as human beings? In essence, there is no closed logical system, purely theoretical, modelled on a geometric ideal of human reason. That view is at odds with the kind of universe we live in. All knowledge is incurably practical. It is active and dynamic, contingent, open-ended and subject to change. All intelligible facts are interpreted, and human judgment is inescapable. Indeed, "the 'practical' dimension of reason is no mere imperfection; it is instead a necessary precondition for there being such a thing as knowledge at all".

Spragens then sets out the hallmarks of a rational society. It will have a large number of rational enterprises, including the sciences, the arts, and the ordering of social relationships. It needs its citizens to be committed to respecting the truth and pursuing the common good—and sustaining a fair degree of consensus on what that common good is. The crucial justification for free speech is that it allows citizens to contribute out of their own experience and expertise to society's grasp of the true and the good. In its public forums, it will therefore demand high standards of argument and justification, and it will give short shrift to the notion that one idea is just as good as any other. Finally, in politics and society, as in private life, rationality is not the only virtue: courage, compassion, altruism and conviviality also have their role to play in the good society.[10]

Alasdair MacIntyre

Alasdair MacIntyre, in a trilogy of books in the 1980s starting with *After Virtue*, similarly starts with a "disquieting suggestion". Our public moral arguments are interminable, principally because there seems no rational way of securing moral agreement. Our moral talk seems to be in a state of disrepair, though we persist in dignifying it with the term "pluralism". But might it be that all we have are fragments of an earlier schema, yet are so myopically immersed in our modern world that we cannot perceive it?[11]

MacIntyre exposes mistakes and incoherences embedded in our technocratic–emotivist culture. First, values are arbitrary; yet that is inconsistent with our common conviction that morality has a claim on us.[12] Secondly, no distinction can be drawn between the exercise of authority and that of sheer power; yet in common parlance authority is reckoned to be the exercise of power which is morally justified.[13] We will therefore constantly be afraid of being manipulated by the will of others, not least by technocrats, since they are focussed on efficiency of means, yet means presuppose ends, and these are arbitrary. Thirdly, there will be no continuity of human identity or character.[14] As Rowan Williams tartly protested in *Lost Icons*, a world of timeless consuming egos, endlessly shape-shifting at every whim, is a social as well as a philosophical shambles.[15] Fourthly, a community will be simply an arena in which individuals pursue their self-chosen conception of the good life, and political institutions exist to provide no more than a framework for that activity. As public debate would lack any rational discussion of values, human passions would readily lead to power struggles and so to violence.[16]

Constructively MacIntyre presents a very different view of persons: "I am my body and my body is social, born to those parents in this community with a specific social identity."[17] So we need to consider the self in relation to our social identities and communal belonging, to know who we are and how individually and corporately we are to guide our actions. MacIntyre thus reflects on concrete historical living in society, and this leads him to the idea of a practice.

Typical examples of a practice are games (consider the ideal of the Olympic Games), the numerous professions, the enquiries of the sciences, the work of the historian, the artist, the dancer, the musician; indeed the whole endeavour of creating and sustaining the culture of human communities. All these are co-operative activities; they are coherent and socially established; and they aim to cultivate the virtues necessary to achieve their proper standards of excellence, and so realize the goods which are internal to them. To attain these skills, you need to accept the rules, be disciplined and be initiated into the standards so far achieved; and also acquire the experience of actually participating in the practice. Only in this way is one likely to achieve excellence, be able to criticize the tradition and even raise the practice to new standards.

Thus the standards are never a matter of preference or taste; they can be rationally discussed within society. Also they are never simply a matter of technical skills, because these serve the goods and ends internal to the practice. Furthermore, one could play games for external goods, such as prestige, status or money, but we normally reserve our praise for the acquisition of the internal goods, and it is in these that the practitioner finds the greatest satisfaction. Moreover, external goods are always some individual's property or possession over against others, whereas internal goods bring benefit for the whole community.[18]

MacIntyre shows how such an understanding of persons, roles and practices found expression in the ancient world, both the Hebrew and the Graeco-Roman, and was largely taken up in the Christian Church, which enlarged and reworked that inheritance, through its distinctive story of Jesus Christ as God's decisive gift to the world. Its understanding of the virtues was made more deeply interior, and it added the crowning theological virtues of faith, hope and love. Christians are citizens of two communities, the earthly and the heavenly, and I may well find there are acute tensions between these two allegiances. But I am never an isolated individual. I belong to an ordered community, in which I am to seek the human good which is also the common good. My end or goal is heavenly, to be sought in this temporal world, where I have no abiding city. I am on a journey or pilgrimage towards redemption.[19]

A crucial question for the viability and vitality of a culture is its capacity to deal with change and crisis. It needs to be able to engage with rival accounts of persons and the world in a constructive, rational manner, and to bring elements together into an enlarged cultural narrative. MacIntyre cites the classic case where Thomas Aquinas, who inhabited the Christian tradition going back to Augustine, was able imaginatively to grasp new developments in knowledge mediated by the Islamic world and so open up a fresh epoch in cultural history.[20]

MacIntyre's verdict is that in contrast the latter-day Enlightenment project is profoundly wanting. Its philosophers were certain that they had discovered a new basis for knowledge, and a set of timeless, universal truths which emancipated them from tradition. Yet at every turn MacIntyre detects a strong connection between their thought and their peculiar social context. He concludes that liberal individualism is as much a tradition as any other. More than that, it is a tradition in deep crisis, and by repudiating the earlier tradition it has deprived itself of the resources to deal constructively with that crisis. For its shrunken concept of technical rationality and its lack of commitment to any set of values means that it possesses no concept of truth which offers a basis for adequate and thorough rational enquiry.[21] MacIntyre does not claim society is totally emotivist. Much of the earlier schema still survives. But technocracy and emotivism threateningly pervade our mindset and permeate every facet of life.

This critique exposes the sheer rootlessness of Hayek's philosophy. Mrs Thatcher was enough of a Conservative to believe in natural roots, but her recourse to an individualistic morality of a Victorian hue was damagingly remote from the experienced reality of millions of ordinary, struggling citizens. Indeed, both Spragens and MacIntyre put down a marker against any ideology which compartmentalizes life, so that there are autonomous areas where power can be exercised exempt from the critical voice of those who have to endure it.

In my Introduction, I showed the threat present in Britain over Parliament, the judiciary, the civil service, the BBC and the very meaning of democracy. All require the sustained practice of reason. By contrast, a technocratic–emotivist approach degrades them into the arbitrary exercise of power, destructive of persons, communities and cultures. For the technocrat claims certain truth where there is only contentious ideology; the emotivist has no concept of truth as a basis for rational enquiry. Politics itself is the rational pursuit of the common good of citizens, yet it becomes both the servant of economic ideology and a succession of manoeuvres to enhance party dominance. In November 2021, the government attempted at a stroke to protect Tory MP Owen Paterson, a serial offender against lobbying rules, force the resignation of the Parliamentary Standards Commissioner, Kathryn Stone, and remodel the independent anti-corruption system.

The prospects are that we shall remain unaware of the nature of our predicament and mired in technocracy–emotivism. The case therefore for finding a new approach is compelling, and it needs to focus on flesh-and-blood persons.

Persons: their loss, defence and primacy

We have reached a central point in our discussion: the loss, defence and primacy of persons. It is crucial here to develop a deep enough understanding of persons. If we equate them with their rational intelligence, the danger remains that most are recast as machines, and then inferior to machines, and so at the mercy of the technocrat to defraud them of their very identity. This is currently of huge importance because of the vast explosion of technology in the digital age, and its very close connection with the free market.

The question of freedom and our human future has been brilliantly and passionately explored by Shoshana Zuboff in *The Age of Surveillance Capitalism: The Fight for a Human Future at the New Frontier of Power*. The phrase "surveillance capitalism" denotes a global system of behaviour modification which threatens human nature. The most powerful players in the digital market like Google and Facebook seek, with or without your permission, to gather every fragment of information about you. In return, they promise to send you highly "personalized" data to match your preferences as part of a seductive "hive" of total connectivity. But you may be unaware that your data are being accumulated into a "behavioural futures market", where predictions about our behaviour are bought and sold. We find ourselves in the crucible of an unprecedented form of power, where there are extreme concentrations of knowledge but there is no democratic oversight. The aim is maximum certainty for maximum profit—for the companies themselves and for the advertisers they know they must retain. But the price is the loss of human freedom. For prediction ends in control. Society is largely oblivious of this massive accumulation of power. Governments are very slow to protect citizens by legislating. Indeed, they are more likely to follow the dogma of free trade, and at the same time enter into collaboration with these vast internet giants for the purpose of surveillance themselves.

The practice of science

It is therefore vital to maintain a rich understanding of persons, in which case we should be able to see how to use artificial intelligence responsibly. This is the place to cut through widespread misunderstanding and get a thorough grip on the nature of the practice of science, and so of the place of technology. I shall first tell the story of Charles Darwin, and then turn to the philosophical reflections of Michael Polanyi.

Charles Darwin

Darwin's enthusiasm for science was inspired first from within his family: his father and grandfather were both medics, the latter with a strong interest in the idea of evolution. At Cambridge University, Charles showed a passion for natural history and was encouraged by the Professor of Botany, J. S. Henslow, who took him on botanical excursions and invited him to his weekly discussion circle. He had only just graduated when in 1831 he was offered a place as naturalist on the survey ship HMS *Beagle*. It was above all the visit to the Galápagos Islands which raised in him a set of fascinating questions about the emergence of different forms of life. He brought back specimens of mockingbirds from four islands. Those from two of the islands appeared to be the same, but the other two were different. He noted that in each island each kind was *exclusively* found. He then remembered being told that the shells of tortoises differed on the various islands: those on lusher islands were rounded, whereas those on drier islands had a peak at the front which enabled them to reach up for higher vegetation. Might it be that the forms of life were not fixed for all time, as Darwin himself had hitherto believed, but could evolve from one form to another? He toyed with the notion of "natural selection" and began tentatively to draw a tree of life.

Darwin was well aware of the wider repercussions his speculations might have within culture. In particular, the direction of his questioning would bring him into sharp conflict with those who believed on the strength of Genesis 1 that God created each species whole and complete. By implication, there could be no change from one species to another. He declined to be drawn in public on his own beliefs, and repeatedly postponed publication. His beloved and devoted wife was also a strong believer who feared for his soul. Eventually, however, his hand was forced. In 1858, Alfred Russel Wallace sent him an essay which set out the same basic ideas as Darwin himself. They were reached entirely independently on the basis of Wallace's extensive researches in Indonesia. And so it was that Darwin's *On the Origin of Species* was finally published in November 1859. The ensuing furore is well known. It was actually more complex than is often thought. Whilst many Christians did doggedly adhere to their preconceptions about Genesis, many attacked his theory out of a prescient fear that "the survival of the fittest" would be used to undermine the integrity of the person—what came to be called "social Darwinism".[22]

Michael Polanyi

This story tallies with Alasdair MacIntyre's account of a practice. It also illustrates much of Michael Polanyi's thesis in his work *Personal Knowledge*. By "personal" he means crucially that it transcends the divide between subjective and objective.[23] In that sense, scientific research is an art. Darwin became an apprentice in a vigorous scientific tradition, learning from those who had themselves become masters of their discipline. To become proficient himself he had at first to submit to the authority of the tradition as a whole and his immediate mentors within it. This is because traditions are forms of practical wisdom. Science students spend much time engaged in practical experiments under the guidance of their mentors. It is only by such engagement that they imbibe the skills and expertise to become proficient themselves. One has to learn, for example, the art of handling and evaluating evidence, and any aspiring researcher has to develop a talent for selecting good questions for investigation. It is only by such development that one graduates from submitting to the authority of one's teachers to relying on one's own judgment. Indeed the student takes on trust and then indwells a whole framework of ideas which are fundamental to the practice of the scientific community and provide an interpretative framework.[24]

In this process, both passion and intellect are deployed. Scientists make a deep personal commitment.[25] The practice of science cannot be expressed in non-committal terms. Of course there is always the risk of error, but there are checks in place, for this commitment is a shared intellectual passion.[26] As Arthur Peacocke pointed out, hypotheses, which are the product of this personal and intellectual commitment, are proposed as inferences to the best explanation. These hypotheses are submitted to the scrutiny of the scientific community so that their truth can be tested. Scientists will ask whether they are internally coherent and consistent; whether they are comprehensive (accounting for more of the known experiences and observations by giving a unified explanation); whether they are cogent and plausible (fitting the best explanation with the established general background); whether they are elegant (as simply expressed as possible, with no undue complexity); and whether they are fruitful in further discoveries.[27] In these ways, the act of intellectual commitment, so far from being purely subjective, actually achieves both subjectivity and objectivity.[28]

Polanyi's approach is a vindication of the capital importance of the imagination and creativity in science—and the same is surely true in mathematics. Thomas Kuhn, in *The Structure of Scientific Revolutions*, showed that science does not develop smoothly by an endless succession of stimulus and response. The idea of natural selection stems from a creative exercise of the imagination: Darwin (and Wallace) reached a radically new way of conceiving the development and relationship of living things. It was an imaginative leap. It forced the scientific community to decide whether this really was a new discovery which necessitated a "paradigm shift", as Kuhn put it, that is, a radical and irreversible change in their accustomed ways of thinking. And, of course, not only the scientific community!

Polanyi was deeply concerned about the symbiosis of scientism and emotivism. He ruthlessly exposed the lethal incoherences of Marxism, from which his native country Hungary suffered.[29] But he is no kinder to the debased liberalism of the West.[30] Its assumptions that there are clear and simple ideas; that knowledge consists in the heaping up of atomic "facts"; that the universe is really only a machine, to be mastered by technical rationality—these are "farcically inadequate". They would include a timetable or a telephone directory among scientific theories.[31] This is the acme of impersonal knowledge, poles apart from the personal knowledge which Polanyi treats as indispensable. So here is a slashing attack on the pursuit of the Holy Grail of impersonal knowledge as the key to meaning: on the contrary, it is self-contradictory and therefore meaningless.[32]

A whole cultural life

Polanyi presses for a right understanding not only of scientific practice in itself, but also of the relation of science to the rest of culture:

Science can ... no longer hope to survive on an island of positive facts, around which the rest of man's intellectual heritage sinks to the status of subjective emotionalism. It must claim that certain emotions are right; and if it can make good such a claim, it will not only save itself but sustain by its example the whole system of cultural life of which it forms part.[33]

Polanyi's insight is brilliantly embodied in the writings of Dava Sobel. Her book *Longitude* tells how Britain offered a prize for solving the technical problem of determining one's position at sea, and John Harrison won it with a series of clocks (which are still on display at Greenwich). But that is inseparable from Harrison's own passionate commitment to his craft, his relations with his family, and the inflexible prejudices of the top brass in the Admiralty, who could not stomach a mere artisan walking off with the prize. Sobel's *Galileo's Daughter* is subtitled *A Drama of Science, Faith and Love*. With deep respect and sympathy, Galileo's intellectual achievements are interwoven with his tenderness for his illegitimate daughter Virginia, who became a nun with the name Suor Maria Celeste. As his body was moved with great ceremony in 1737 to his present resting place in the Church of Santa Croce, a second body was discovered to have been buried with him: it was his beloved daughter. And still she is there—but there is no inscription to announce her presence. In her book *The Planets*, Sobel imaginatively fuses science, history, biography, poetry and storytelling.

Our social divisions: women, men and children

With such writers to guide us, I now turn to various social divisions in our culture which present a deep challenge.

Elaine Graham highlighted a weakness in the Enlightenment project, in that it was a manifesto for the self-actualization of the male subject. It set up binary and gendered constructions of culture and nature: the male is awarded the plums of rational enquiry, the public arena, and an autonomous human destiny; the female is considered non-rational, confined to the private domestic arena, and consigned to dependency.[34]

How, Graham wonders, are we to encourage practices which overcome these dichotomies and reach for the full humanity of persons, women and men together?

It is a laudable aim, but once again we encounter technology wizards keen to satisfy the consumer market. Jenny Kleeman gives us a graphic portrait of the sex robot industry, which seeks to sate the desires of men who cannot relate to, or actively loathe, women. It will either provide warmth and comfort to socially isolated men or allow misogynist incels (involuntary celibates) to live out their rape fantasies. Now they can meet Harmony, who is available at a considerable price to be friend, lover and even life partner. The industry is run by men with global market ambitions. Kleeman concludes that the rise of the sex robot is not just about the objectification of women. It is a humanist as much as a feminist problem. The digital revolution has left us less prepared for face-to-face interactions, less able to relate in the real world. If I can own a partner purely to please me—without the bother of in-laws, menstrual cycles, emotional baggage or independent ambitions—my capacity to relate to others will be diminished. If empathy is no longer needed, we will all be a little less human.[35]

This is the place to face the issue of child sexual exploitation. Crucial for any country is the treatment of children. They need protection from all forms of invasion of their person through the years when they are growing to maturity. For fourteen years, I was secretary to a charity and company opposing child sexual exploitation. It started when my wife and I heard that Irene Ivison, a friend of my sister, had lost her daughter Fiona at the age of seventeen. She had lost her first to a man who had groomed her for sex, and then to a punter who murdered her. The second man confessed and served nine years of a life sentence. The first was never brought to book, though Irene said he was the real killer.

Irene thought at first that Fiona was an isolated victim, but soon discovered that child sexual exploitation was rife, affecting people from every walk of life. She took a writer's course to enable her to produce *Fiona's Story: A Tragedy of our Times*. She also founded the charity, now known as Parents Against Child Exploitation (Pace) UK. The staff focus on supporting the parents of children who are already exploited or at risk of exploitation by someone outside the family. We produced a booklet making them aware of the grooming process. One member of staff relates specially to government, advising on proposed legislation. We were deeply involved in the overhaul of sexual offences legislation by Home Secretary David Blunkett in 2002. We also knew of the inaction of the police and the collusion of local politicians in Rotherham ten years before Professor Alexis Jay's revelations in 2012.

Two occasions stay in my mind. On one occasion, during a local consultation, one delegate, visibly embarrassed by the whole subject, immediately applied an individual morality and blamed the girls for failing to say "no" to being groomed. When we pointed out the difficulties for a twelve-year-old in resisting an older man, he then blamed her parents for failing to impress on the girl the necessity of saying "no". It was often hard to convince well-intentioned people of the skill of the perpetrators in deflecting attention from their criminal activity.

The second occasion was at our national conference. A crucial ingredient of these conferences was to stay with parents' lived experience of child sexual exploitation and to let people tell it as it really was. An anguished mother came forward to tell how she had lost her child to a man who had mercilessly groomed her. She complained that social services, to whom she had repeatedly turned, had in the end told her that her child had made her life-choice, and that she should let her go. She could not possibly do so. Behind the attitude of social services was not some negative moral rule, but the modern Western notion, which we have already seen MacIntyre repudiate, that we are really individual atoms who have to claim our freedom and autonomy, and any relationships worth having are entirely self-chosen. The mother knew otherwise but was utterly powerless. It was only through being able to find a listening ear and pour out her anguish that she could sense any empowerment or hope.

Our global role

I noted earlier Peter Frankopan's observation that the Western powers harnessed technical invention to their global ambitions. Europe has for centuries been aggressive, both internally and externally. President Putin's war on Ukraine is a stark tragedy, utterly indefensible in its basis and method. His mindset is a native brew of memories, grievances and aspirations: Russia's imperial destiny under an autocrat; past invasions, especially by Napoleon and Hitler; victory over Nazism in the "Great Patriotic War"; the humiliating disintegration of Russia as a superpower. There are ethnic and religious overtones: Russians and Ukrainians are "one people", inhabiting "one Rus'", the holy territory of Orthodoxy centred on Kyiv and Moscow; there is the centuries-old suffering of an almost Christ-like people. Liberalism is spurned as poisonously degenerate, spreading eastwards, along with NATO, and menacing the very life of Russia. No wonder Putin discourages any critical reflection on Stalin's reign of terror and suppresses organizations memorializing his victims as unpatriotic. Ukraine is to be purged of its "neo-Nazism" and reabsorbed by any means and at any cost: language is corrupted, truth and lies are inverted, and ordinary people, even Putin's own, are subject to repression and terror, mere pawns in an apocalyptic struggle. Putin is matched by Strelnikov (Pasha Antipov in Boris Pasternak's *Doctor Zhivago*), who uses wanton violence to purge a whole culture of impurity.

We in the West must find the wisdom to aid the victims and counter that mindset as best we can in a nuclear age. It is a sign of hope that there is a widespread determination to move beyond the old aggression. This is experimentally embedded in the European Union, which for all its failings is based on the model of a Europe of equal, independent democratic states respecting the rule of law, committed to resolving all disputes by peaceful means, and collaborating with each other. We need to pursue and commend the highest possible standards of humanity. As of March 2022, it remains to be seen whether we can find paths towards shared diverse cultural goods right across Europe and a just and lasting peace. So I turn to the global role of Britain.

In the case of the British, geography has played a major role. Even as a United Kingdom of four countries we are very small. But as if to offset the potential disadvantage, we are detached from mainland Europe, if only by a few miles of sea. Our most famous bard put into the mouth of John of Gaunt a paean to

> This royal throne of kings, this scepter'd isle,
> This earth of majesty, this seat of Mars,
> This other Eden...
> This fortress built by Nature for herself
> Against infection and the hand of war,
> This happy breed of men...
> This precious stone set in the silver sea,
> Which serves it in the office of a wall...
> Against the envy of less happier lands,
> This blessed plot, this earth, this realm, this England,
> This nurse, this teeming womb of royal kings...
> Renowned for their deeds as far from home,
> For Christian service and true chivalry.[36]

It is quite irresistible. One so easily misses the sleight of hand that England is said to be an isle—which raises vast questions about today's state of the Union.

Here is the charter for the Englishman's natural sense of effortless superiority and for England's imperial destiny. Actually John of Gaunt's rosy rhetoric is punctured by Thomas Piketty's exposition of the era of ownership societies, based on the sanctity of private property and wealth, where the ruling class has always had to struggle with how to reconcile the rest of society to this ideology. The English ruling elite have been remarkably successful in maintaining their status and inducing acquiescence and support among the lower orders. John Harrison's experience (and Elizabeth Bennet's!) anticipated the tart remarks of R. H. Tawney: as long as they are masters of the situation, they are all kindness and condescension, but question their credentials and the lamb becomes a lion, roaring in grief and indignation, defending its bone to the last.[37]

In his coruscating book *Heroic Failure*, the Irish writer Fintan O'Toole has explored the most recent expression of English nationalism in the mentality of those on the right who drove through a hard Brexit. He sees Brexit as an essentially English phenomenon. We find a curious combination of an unshakeable sense of superiority in pursuit of imperial nationalism, yet also a sense of grievance at imaginary intolerable oppression by the EU, the two being oddly yoked together by the pleasurable emotion of self-pity. We find buccaneering deregulated capitalism twinned with an incontinent emotivist approach to our historical relations with our European neighbours.[38]

The English have never been much inclined to look self-critically at their imperial and colonial history, whilst fully expecting others to repent of theirs. It is as if historical truth can be ignored if it does not support our self-congratulatory narrative. Today, whilst in one sense we have got Brexit done, in another sense, because it is based primarily in ideology and mood, it readily becomes an endless emotive crusade for the Holy Grail of absolute sovereignty and freedom, without rational connection with reality in terms of sustained and consistent strategy or policy.

The British have been in a state of rivalry with continental powers for centuries. As they expanded their empire round the globe, they may have acquired some respect for the cultures they came to dominate, but it was always laced with condescension and never got in the way of the commercial interests of the British. Whole cultures were destined to be remodelled to the British template. The British did believe that the Indians were entitled to the just operation of (British) law; but it never crossed their minds that India had a right not to be ruled by the British at all. They had some respect for the venerable culture of China, but when in 1839 the Chinese Emperor tried to curb the flow of opium grown in India, the British were incensed that the universal axiom of free trade was being violated and went to war. They outgunned the Chinese and forced them in 1841 to cede Hong Kong, and then clapped an unequal trade treaty on them.

The Japanese learned the lesson. They banned all Westerners from the country early in the seventeenth century, and when they were forced in 1853 to relate to the outside world (the Americans dropped by with demands for a deal), they became wholly determined to preserve their own cultural heritage and to learn from the West all that was necessary to maintain their independence. They adapted Bismarck's constitution and transformed their emperor into a constitutional monarch whilst leaving him divine father of the children of Japan. They acquired the technical knowledge of armaments to defend themselves by shrewdly commending themselves to Lord Armstrong of Cragside. And so, in perfect imitation, they finally unleashed a war to rid East Asia of Western imperialism once and for all.

When I was a boy, the Germans were almost our gentlemanly enemies, whereas the Japanese were absolute fiends. I naturally tended to take in the verdict. As it happens, I have had occasion to travel most of all to Germany and Japan, and have had the privilege of coming to know Germans and Japanese as colleagues and friends. It is sad that ignorant stereotypes are still so widespread.

But the British sense of superiority bore most heavily on black people. David Olusoga's TV programmes (based on his book *Black and British: A Forgotten History*) have revealed how deeply our imperial history is entangled with the slave trade. Back in the seventeenth century, a British company had the monopoly of the slave trade in West Africa. One patron was the Duke of York, the future James II, whose initials DY were branded onto slaves held for export.[39] This monopoly was challenged in the courts by independent entrepreneurs. They won. After all, along with property nothing was more sacrosanct in English law than the doctrine of free trade. The new slave traders fully exercised the economic virtue of efficiency and elevated the practice to an industrial scale.[40] Men, women and their children had no rights at all and were subjected to appalling regimes, with the rape of women at will; sadism was interlaced with misogyny. If the slaves had the temerity to rebel, they were crushed with great ferocity.[41]

The British were, it is true, the first to outlaw slavery in their territories. It is perhaps less well known that victory for Wilberforce and his colleagues was not achieved through moral revulsion that people should be enslaved. Once again the sanctity of property prevailed; for as a precondition for passing the abolition bill the government had to commit itself to a scheme compensating the slave owners for their loss. A project within University College London has shown just how widespread slave ownership was: 46,000 claims for compensation were recognized, from all walks of life; for many widows it was their only means of income. The total pay-out ran to about £17bn in today's money and it came to an end only in 2015. Much of the money went into more opulent homes, family inheritance, and investments in the City of London for all kinds of enterprises and of infrastructure. Thus our ability to remain ahead of our rivals in the imperial stakes relied heavily on profit from the slave trade.[42]

Following Abolition, the British displayed a sense of moral superiority and set about militarily stopping other nations trading in slaves. The movement was always shot through with self-interest and soon became entangled in the American Civil War and in the colonization of Africa. Cecil Rhodes had the ambition to build a railway line from Cape Town to Cairo which would run entirely through British-controlled territory. In 1895, three African kings could see that this would mean a strip of exclusively British development along the line, with black people reduced to indentured labourers on either side. As they were already Christian gentlemen, they thought they might be able to win over the British public and pressurize the government. They spent three months on their campaign, and finally persuaded the government to stop Rhodes in his tracks. It was a rare victory.[43] Right up to the 1950s, Africans were still being looked upon mainly as children needing European parental control.

Normally, if any black people came to Britain, at best they were treated with great condescension, at worst with suspicion and hostility: they were to be kept in their proper place, and in accordance with the law of the "slippery slope" not given any chance to "swamp" the country. Eventually Britain needed their labour, and so, from 1948, the Windrush generation came to settle. Their recent scandalous treatment by the Home Office under its "hostile environment" policy is of a piece with this long history of discrimination against black people.

The considerations I have set out here are but a fraction of the evidence which all needs sifting for an honest and truthful interpretation to be made. Unfortunately it is quite clear that the government is playing culture war over Britain's colonial and imperial past. Those who seek critical scrutiny were denigrated by the former Communities Secretary, Robert Jenrick, as "baying mobs" and "mindless destroyers" of "our shared British history". The issue of the truth or legitimacy of the past is reconfigured as a matter of present law and order. The former Culture Secretary, Oliver Dowden, told heritage and culture bodies that countries should not "run from or airbrush the history upon which they are founded", and that the government's ambition is to "retain and explain" statues with chequered histories. He explicitly said he expected them to follow the government's position, and in at least one case threatened its public funding.[44]

The response of Prime Minister Johnson and Conservative MPs to the acquittal of the "Colston Four" purported to be impeccably factual and logical ("You cannot retrospectively change our history", "Criminal damage is criminal damage") and the Attorney General (no less) darkly claimed there was "confusion" which required the law to be clarified. But it is they who are causing the confusion, whether deliberately or instinctively. Of course what is done cannot be undone. But persons constantly evaluate history, and rightly so, since they hope to learn from it and become more human. In this particular case, a person, Edward Colston, enslaved as many as 84,000 persons, men, women and children, of whom about 19,000 died. The jury was entitled to evaluate this conduct and decide that there was a lawful case for damaging his statue. Actually the government had already made its own uncritical appraisal of British colonial and imperial history, and was bent on deploying its political power to control the narrative and denigrate all others, whilst prating about the defence of freedom. This is the current expression of the hoary ideological credo that the Conservative Party is the natural party of government. Its approach is emotivist, replete with mischievously manipulable terms like "woke" and "the blob", to keep fuelling a populist culture war. For it is about the irrational consolidation of power, and it discounts the numerous social forums where important issues are debated within a democratic system. The Policing Act is consistent with this outlook; for it criminalizes many forms of protest, and in any case many extra clauses were inserted after its passage through the House of Commons. Jonathan Sumption's diagnosis and foreboding which I set out in the Introduction is entirely justified: rampant populism is ousting parliamentary democracy. Actually any democratic society of the sort Thomas A. Spragens set out should be mature enough openly and rationally to examine its inevitably ambivalent past.

This emotivism is increasingly aligned with the populist press, which has long followed the Harmsworth brothers' recipe for commercial success: "The British people relish a good hero and a good hate."[45] It is also matched by the ethos of social media, which is endlessly reinforced by the "like" button. Here people tend to select one issue and relentlessly pursue it. So we have increasingly bitter assaults as one person (often unwittingly) falls foul of another's crusade. Social media are ideal for this kind of warfare. Postings are instantly accessible to millions, so provide a never-ending source of targets. And the vigilante can lob grenades incognito from a distant bunker.

Rather than that, other approaches are far more promising. I turn to an artist who knows what it is to be "othered", even by his fellow Jews, and whose sensitivity, passion and insight may provide much that we need for our healing.

Music and life: everything is connected

Daniel Barenboim is a world-class pianist and conductor. He has pondered deeply the practice of music-making and its relation to life, and is remarkably articulate on the subject. I shall draw especially on his book *Everything is Connected: The Power of Music*. The topics within it are the result of almost sixty years of performance, instruction and contemplation.[46] A major stimulus for him was his great friendship with Professor Edward Said, of Palestinian origin. Said became Barenboim's "soulmate",[47] and the two of them produced a record of their conversations in *Parallels and Paradoxes: Explorations in Music and Society* (edited by Ara Guzelimian).

Barenboim points out that though music is obviously sound, sound in itself is not yet music. When one makes music, all the elements have to be integrated into an organic whole. In music, everything must be constantly and permanently interconnected: rhythm, melody, harmony, tempo, volume, all are interdependent. Moreover, in music, sound is limited in time. Sound emerges from silence and dies away back into silence. In this respect, music is a mirror of life, which also starts and ends in nothing.[48] These themes pervade the two books.

Together Barenboim and Said created the West-Eastern Divan Orchestra to bring together musicians of Jewish and Arab origin.

Barenboim and Said are both very concerned with the mirror images of homogenization and xenophobia, which tend to resist any mediation between them. Both generate a fear of "the other".[49] Said strongly believed that separation between people is not a solution for any of the problems which divide us, and ignorance of the other provides no help whatsoever. Dialogue is essential, and music itself is a dialogue. Their intention was to find common ground between estranged peoples. If young musicians could agree on how to play even one note together, they would not be able to look at each other in the same way again. For the art of playing music is that of simultaneous playing and listening, the one enhancing the other. And this takes place on both an individual and a collective level.[50]

Through music it is possible to envisage an alternative social model. Barenboim and Said believe that the destinies of the Palestinians and the Israelis are inextricably linked, and therefore the welfare, dignity and happiness of the one must inevitably be that of the other. Of course the West-Eastern Divan Orchestra is not able to bring about peace:

> It can, however, create the conditions for understanding without which it is impossible even to speak of peace. It has the potential to awaken the curiosity of each individual to listen to the narrative of the other and to inspire the courage necessary to hear what one would prefer not to ... True acceptance ... means to acknowledge the difference and dignity of the other.

And that entails recognizing their freedom, individuality and equality.[51] It was these convictions which inspired the orchestra's courageous step in August 2005 of giving a concert in Ramallah, where Barenboim had already given recitals.

Barenboim is eloquent about the vital importance of artists in times of totalitarian rule. Culture, in this context, has frequently been the only avenue of independent thought, the only way people can meet as equals and exchange ideas freely. It becomes the primary voice of the oppressed and takes over from politics as a driving force for change, influencing the collective consciousness of the people. Barenboim himself has a long association with the Staatskapelle Berlin and believes that the intensity of their playing is a testimony to their having lived under both Nazism and Communism, which fostered their realization that music was like oxygen, since this was the one place where they could really be free.[52]

He also has a catalogue of strictures on Western society. The advantage of confrontation with a totalitarian regime is that it is easy to identify your enemy. The threat in the West is far more insidious. I am reminded of Alasdair MacIntyre's closing observation in *After Virtue* that new dark ages are already upon us; indeed the barbarians have been governing us for quite some time; and it is our lack of consciousness of this that constitutes part of our predicament.[53]

In the world of education, the study of music is often ignored or treated as of little significance:

> Education means preparing children for adult life; teaching them how to behave and what kinds of human beings they want to be. Everything else is information and can be learned in a very simple way. To play music well you need to strike a balance between your head, your heart and your stomach... What better way than music to show a child how to be human?[54]

Barenboim complains bitterly about "muzak", piped music which assails our ears everywhere, so that we hear music but do not listen to it. It is simply there for emotional purposes. It is the greatest hindrance to the integration of music into our society. It is of course widely used to sell products. Barenboim gives the instance of a commercial which used the *Lacrimosa* from Mozart's *Requiem* to sell toilets. When the company received complaints, they assumed that the objection was to religious blasphemy. So they promised to replace it with Wagner's Tannhäuser Overture, since they had been assured it was not religious. No, declares Barenboim, the misuse of music is absolutely offensive—in musical terms. Using fragments of great works of music to infiltrate popular culture cannot be the solution to the crisis in classical music. Accessibility does not come through populism, but through greater interest, curiosity and knowledge. For music requires silence and total concentration on the part of the listener. As Barenboim pithily puts it, muzak replaces participation of the intellect with passive consumption.[55]

Barenboim and Said's criticisms largely hinge on the concept of knowledge. Nowadays schools and universities give much more information and much less education. There seems to be an assumption that if you divide a piece of music or anything else into tinier and tinier units, then you can suddenly put it all together. We are dogged by increasing specialization and the fragmentation of knowledge. This weakens communication between people and plays into the hands of so-called technocratic experts. There is here a certain kind of ideological indoctrination, as if it's not your problem, and somebody else will solve it for you.[56]

Another problem is the slogan and the soundbite. This is "part of the mentality of our age—that everything is made compact, reduced to a token or a slogan. . . . It's as if you would say: 'Well, give me the essence of Beethoven's score in two minutes.'" Barenboim contrasts "ideology" with "idea". Ideologies are strategies for getting an idea implemented, but they oversimplify ideas into closed rules and systems. Ideas have an open content, and content demands a particular amount of time, which you cannot compress. Ideas involve choosing to re-examine one's principles rather than being satisfied with a pre-packaged solution, and they challenge both intellect and character. That in turn requires discipline, and "that discipline involves knowing something, having a particular culture, having a particular training". Barenboim detects a "contradiction in the fact that we live in an age that considers itself extremely critical but does not require of the individual to have the means to criticize".[57]

The net result is a monumental ignorance in society. It confuses choice with freedom. Freedom requires a keen awareness of one's appetites, otherwise "one is simply the slave of these appetites and not in possession of the power to shape one's own ideas and actions". Moreover, people are not well versed in either the sciences or the arts. They are unable to think beyond the present and the immediate future to understand fully the consequences of political action.[58] Equally they have little interest in history, and indeed little curiosity about the world of today. They want above all to feel good. They are therefore wide open to exploitation and manipulation. As Edward Said says, there is no point in making people feel good: "I've always been very interested not so much in making people comfortable but in making them uncomfortable. There are certain questions to be raised; there are certain attitudes to be addressed; in the end, there are certain clichés that you want to dismantle."[59]

All this bodes no good for a democratic society. Unless politicians are genuine statesmen (perhaps a Nelson Mandela), they are only fixers, when what is needed is the intellectual's and the artist's vision and strategy and their courageous refusal to compromise. Thus Edward Said says that for him, "a very important part of the practice of music is that music, in some profound way, is perhaps the final resistance to ... the commodification of everything".[60]

So Barenboim and Said expose Westerners' delusion that by dividing life into atomic bits of information they will find knowledge, and by giving individuals boundless choice they will find freedom. Internationally Barenboim and Said reject separation and isolation. Against this, at the most fundamental level, they advance the notion of wholeness. Both in music and in life, the whole is much more than the sum of the parts. Everything is connected, so the musician has at the very least to learn to group notes and search for and understand each part of the music in terms of the ultimate nature of the whole.[61] It is no surprise therefore that when Said laments the disappearance of wholeness in society, he uses the phrase "structural wholeness".[62] Structure cannot be one more atomic thing, to be bolted on to all the other atoms. It is crucial to the coherence and meaning simultaneously of the whole and of the several elements. Barenboim learned, through seeking musical coherence and meaning, the relationship of the individual and the group in society. Just as for orchestral unity each part must express itself conscious of its relation to the whole and every other part, so the human being is to contribute to society in a very individual way through being conscious of the greater whole. "This, of course, is much easier to achieve in music than in life."[63]

Crucial here is a deep sense of our common life, if we are genuinely to communicate with each other. Barenboim and Said both recognize the intensity, courage and struggle of Beethoven. He is able to communicate with everyone, regardless of race or class, in a common discourse. The Choral Symphony is all about a certain kind of affirmation, which powerfully connects with the affirmation of the human being in society and with promises of liberation and fulfilment in a shared common life.[64]

Artistic knowledge: spiralling creativity and gratuitous excess

Daniel Barenboim reveals the intensely personal character of musical knowledge. Of course, this would be disqualified in some Enlightenment circles, but if we go by MacIntyre's idea of a practice, then the arts are also forms of public knowledge. They just have a rather different logic. It is imperative not to practise reductionism, whereby one form of knowledge is collapsed into another. Mathematics and scientific knowledge are perfectly valid in their own spheres. But artistic knowledge is equally valid. Just how it is different is shown in a discussion by Rowan Williams.

Rowan Williams is a poet and interpreter of literature (particularly Dostoevsky) as well as a theologian. In *Grace and Necessity: Reflections on Art and Love*, he has explored the writings of the French Catholic philosopher Jacques Maritain, the Welsh poet and painter David Jones, and the American novelist Flannery O'Connor. He throws a flood of light on our ways of knowing.

He is well aware that it is fashionable in latter-day Enlightenment thought to start out from the idea of the individual as an inner, free subject over against a mechanical universe. The individual receives stimuli from objects out there, abstracts them from the process of time, and makes sense of them by labelling them. Williams disagrees with these assumptions on every count. In the first place, we live a shared, common life in communities, which change within a changing world across time. Williams claims that this is the context within which all our knowing takes place: truthfulness unfolds within time. So we do not come to know by freezing an object. Rather the whole human system of knowing is inescapably mobile, what he calls a spiral of self-extending symbolic activity. That is, knowledge is so much more than general abstractions. It involves the use of symbols, and one set of symbolic clues by one person generates in turn another set of moves by another. What is enacted and seen in one place is lived again in another, so knowing involves not so much the labelling of an object as the re-enacting of a performance. This is in response to reality itself, which is a mobile, dynamic pattern whose best analogy is not mechanical but musical.

Williams sees art as an acute case of our knowing in general, a manifestation of the deeper levels of participatory knowledge. The artist responds to the dynamic and generative capacity of the world to create a work. This work not only has a life of its own, but in turn generates further responses, either from the same artist (we may think of Monet compulsively painting haystacks) or another (Milton and Blake influencing Philip Pullman), often in another medium (as Alphonse de Lamartine's poetry inspired some of Franz Liszt's most glorious piano works). Williams sees here a gratuitous excess inherent in the universe, something which art approaches, but never controls.

The modern world, says Williams, is prone to take instrumental thinking as its model, manipulating objects to solve practical problems. There is of course a place for this in life, but if it is seen as the only model, then art, which has no obvious utility value, and indeed a strong element of playfulness, is bound to seem only idle or arbitrary, merely an expression of the emotions or the will, and devoid of any intellectual content. Yet in fact artists testify to the hard work involved in creating. As they seek to bring into being a particular work, they struggle with the logic of their vision of what is there. To ensure the integrity of the work, they find they need to obey. They often experience a drivenness, even a self-dispossession. There is a kind of necessity in the thing being made, underlying the contingency of the world that has been truthfully imagined. Observing this integrity can be said to be the mode of the artist's love.[65]

Thus there is no one form of rationality, nor is there just the dual form of mathematical and scientific reasoning. There are multiple forms, and the whole patently has an open texture which allows for inexhaustible creativity and gratuitous excess. And that is because of the generative and creative capacities of persons, who in turn live lives which are responsive to the generative capacities of the universe itself. This means we face a huge challenge. We have not only to exorcize the demons of technocracy-emotivism and culture wars, but also to recognize the diversity and complexity of the world around us, and engage openly and rationally, imaginatively and passionately with one another, whilst preserving and pursuing some deeper sense of our unity. It is with this unity-in-diversity that I shall be particularly concerned in the remainder of this book.

Notes

1. In an interview in *Woman's Own*, 31 October 1987.
2. See e.g. Milton Friedman, *Capitalism and Freedom*; Friedrich A. Hayek, *The Road to Serfdom;* Friedrich A. Hayek, *Law, Legislation and Liberty, Vol. 2: The Mirage of Social Justice*, esp. pp. 96f.
3. Michael J. Sandel, *A New Citizenship*, Lecture 4: "A New Politics of the Common Good". BBC Reith Lectures for 2009.
4. Peter Frankopan, *The Silk Roads: A New History of the World*, pp. 243–63.
5. Thomas A. Spragens, Jr, *The Irony of Liberal Reason*, p. vii.
6. Spragens, *The Irony of Liberal Reason*, pp. vii–viii.
7. Spragens, *The Irony of Liberal Reason*, pp. 27–31, 48, 70.
8. Spragens, *The Irony of Liberal Reason*, pp. 55–68, 89–127; quotation from Descartes on p. 56.
9. Spragens, *The Irony of Liberal Reason*, e.g. pp. 202f.
10. Spragens, *The Irony of Liberal Reason*, summary of Chapters 8 and 9; quotation on p. 355.
11. Alasdair MacIntyre, *After Virtue: A Study in Moral Theory*, pp. 1–10.
12. MacIntyre, *After Virtue*, pp. 41–50.
13. MacIntyre, *After Virtue*, pp. 26, 30, 74.
14. MacIntyre, *After Virtue*, pp. 23f.
15. Rowan Williams, *Lost Icons: Reflections on Cultural Bereavement*, p. 49.
16. MacIntyre, *After Virtue*, pp. 71, 195.
17. MacIntyre, *After Virtue*, p. 172.
18. MacIntyre, *After Virtue*, pp. 187f.
19. MacIntyre, *After Virtue*, pp. 169–73.
20. Alasdair MacIntyre, *Whose Justice? Which Rationality?*, Chapters 9–10; Alasdair MacIntyre, *Three Rival Versions of Moral Enquiry*, Chapters 4–6.
21. MacIntyre, *Whose Justice? Which Rationality?*, pp. 367–9.
22. This account draws especially on David Attenborough's BBC programme to mark the bicentenary of Charles Darwin's birth, 1 February 2009.
23. Michael Polanyi, *Personal Knowledge: Towards a Post-Critical Philosophy*, p. 300, cf. p. 17.
24. Polanyi, *Personal Knowledge*, pp. 30, 53–60.
25. Polanyi, *Personal Knowledge*, pp. 65, 61.
26. Polanyi, *Personal Knowledge*, pp. 264–6.

27 Arthur R. Peacocke, *Paths from Science towards God: The End of all our Exploring*, pp. 27f.
28 Polanyi, *Personal Knowledge*, pp. 5, 63f., 311, cf. 300.
29 Polanyi, *Personal Knowledge*, pp. 227–330.
30 Polanyi, *Personal Knowledge*, pp. 237f.
31 Polanyi, *Personal Knowledge*, p. 267, cf. p. 9.
32 Polanyi, *Personal Knowledge*, p. 253.
33 Polanyi, *Personal Knowledge*, p. 134.
34 Elaine Graham, *Between a Rock and a Hard Place: Public Theology in a Post-Secular Age*, p. 54.
35 Jenny Kleeman, *Sex Robots and Vegan Meat: Adventures at the Frontier of Birth, Food, Sex & Death*, pp. 14–27, 87f.
36 William Shakespeare, *The Tragedy of King Richard the Second*, Act II, Scene I, lines 40–54.
37 R. H. Tawney, *Equality*, pp. 37–9.
38 Fintan O'Toole, *Heroic Failure: Brexit and the Politics of Pain*, pp. xvii, 3, 82.
39 David Olusoga, *Black and British: A Forgotten History*, pp. 22f.
40 Olusoga, *Black and British*, pp. 73–6.
41 See Olusoga, *Black and British*, p. 229 for an example.
42 Olusoga, *Black and British*, pp. 229–32.
43 Olusoga, *Black and British*, pp. 413–9.
44 Charlotte Higgins, "Taking down statues is not 'censorship'", *The Guardian*, 21 January 2021, Opinion p. 4; Peter Walker, "New appointment to stop spread of 'woke' culture on campuses", *The Guardian*, 15 February 2021, p. 13; Jim Waterson, "Oliver Dowden: The paymaster who is calling the tune in the culture wars", *The Guardian*, 12 June 2021, p. 22.
45 <https://spartacus-educational.com/spartacus-blogURL101.htm> 19 February 2018, accessed 15 March 2022.
46 Daniel Barenboim, *Everything is Connected: The Power of Music*, p. 4.
47 Barenboim, *Everything is Connected*, p. 155.
48 Barenboim, *Everything is Connected*, pp. 7–15.
49 Daniel Barenboim and Edward Said, *Parallels and Paradoxes: Explorations in Music and Society*, p. 152.
50 Barenboim, *Everything is Connected*, pp. 65f.
51 Barenboim, *Everything is Connected*, pp. 68–74.

52 Barenboim, *Everything is Connected*, pp. 62f., 72; Barenboim and Said, *Parallels and Paradoxes*, p. 147.
53 MacIntyre, *After Virtue*, p. 263.
54 Barenboim and Said, *Parallels and Paradoxes*, p. 24.
55 Barenboim, *Everything is Connected*, pp. 3, 39–42.
56 Barenboim and Said, *Parallels and Paradoxes*, pp. 64, 14, 149.
57 Barenboim and Said, *Parallels and Paradoxes*, pp. 57f.; Barenboim, *Everything is Connected*, p. 48.
58 Barenboim, *Everything is Connected*, pp. 45f., 56.
59 Barenboim and Said, *Parallels and Paradoxes*, pp. 149, 78.
60 Barenboim and Said, *Parallels and Paradoxes*, pp. 60, 168.
61 Barenboim, *Everything is Connected*, pp. 11, 53.
62 Barenboim and Said, *Parallels and Paradoxes*, p. 148.
63 Barenboim, *Everything is Connected*, pp. 11, 62.
64 Barenboim and Said, *Parallels and Paradoxes*, pp. 143–50.
65 Rowan Williams, *Grace and Necessity: Reflections on Art and Love*, section Four, esp. pp. 135–53.

PART 2

Western Christianity

In Part 1, I deliberately avoided reference to the role of Christianity in our culture. I was keen at that stage to make critiques and proposals which were humanistic and did not rest on explicit Christian assumptions. Part 2 considers our Western Christian inheritance, in a quest to identify the forms of Christianity which best support and ground those humanistic proposals. The journey will take us back to ancient Greek philosophy, especially Plato, and then we will examine how Western Christians have related Christ both to their Hebrew inheritance and also to the Graeco-Roman. I shall conclude by commending the dialogic approach of William Temple and the integralist approach of Henri de Lubac, setting out the basic stance of the latter. All this will prepare the ground for Part 3 and Part 4.

Jeremy Lent

I will conduct that quest by responding to a fascinating book by Jeremy Lent, *The Patterning Instinct: A Cultural History of Humanity's Search for Meaning.* He surveys a vast range of different people: early hunter-gatherers and farmers, the Egyptians, ancient Greek philosophers, traditional Chinese sages, the rise of Christianity, the trailblazers of the Scientific Revolution, and those who constructed our consumer society. He identifies the root metaphors that cultures have used to construct meaning in their world. He shows how mediaeval Christian rationalism acted as an incubator for scientific thought, which in turn shaped our modern vision of the conquest of nature. He is especially concerned with our current ecological crisis of unsustainability. He believes that this is not an inevitable result of our human nature but is actually culturally driven: it is a product of mental patterns that could conceivably be reshaped. He foresees a struggle between two contrasting views of humanity. One is driving us to a technological endgame of artificially enhanced humans. The other enables a sustainable future arising from our intrinsic connectedness with each other and the natural world. This struggle is one in which each of us will play a role through the meaning we forge from the lives we lead.

This approach has affinities with that adopted in Part 1: Lent focusses on lived experience and our responses to it, in the face of ideologies constructed to manage our corporate and individual lives. He sees whole cultures as practices in a MacIntyrean sense. He is multi-disciplinary, taking seriously the various disciplines which have emerged in the course of our history. He has a deep sense of the need to go far upstream to unearth the sources of our current habits of thought. He focusses on central issues of our times and seeks a true understanding of humanity. And he believes that this is a task for us all: indeed we shall play a part for good or ill, whether we exert ourselves or not.

His book is all the more fascinating because it gives an account of Christianity as manifestly a major part of our cultural predicament, and in no way offering a solution. In fact he is attracted primarily to Chinese ways of approaching the question of meaning in our lives. Since Christianity claims to be a world religion and has always undertaken evangelization and mission, Lent confronts Christians with the very serious task of examining their self-understanding across the centuries.

I need therefore to spell out the challenge posed by Jeremy Lent. According to his account, the West is heir both to the Hebrew and the Graeco-Roman civilizations. In the fifth and fourth centuries BC, stimulated by seafaring and trade in goods and ideas, the Greek civilization flowered to give us new ways of thinking: philosophy, democracy, tragedy, logic and mathematics and the practice of systematic and empirical thinking. One feature of what makes us uniquely human is our capacity for symbolic thought. Lent says, "By creating higher-level generalizations from a mass of concrete specifics, symbolic thought permitted language to evolve and drove the development of early humanity's mythic consciousness ... Abstracting a general rule from an assortment of details is the defining characteristic of Greek thought." The Greeks took this to an entirely new level of sophistication. Things made more sense to the Greeks the more they were part of a general theory. They were not content to speak of things being good; they wanted to know what "*the* Good" was. This was the birth of the very idea of abstraction.[1]

I shall focus first on Lent's presentation of Plato, and then on his account of Christianity. I will say in advance that in the case of Plato, Lent rather oversimplifies, which is understandable in such an ambitious project. Plato had a long life (427–347 BC), and his thinking subtly developed. In any case, so much is conveyed through the mouth of his revered mentor Socrates. So there is no easy answer to the question of what Plato believed. However, Lent is right to make much of Plato's dualism, which is both cosmological and runs through every person in the relation of body to soul. And it is on dualism that I wish to focus. In the case of Christianity, Lent clearly believes it is quite simply dualistic. This dualism was mainly derived from Platonism, and over the centuries it grew in intensity. I recognize the powerful tendency among Western Christians towards dualism, and Lent gives copious evidence. Yet Western Christianity has in fact been quite diverse in its estimate of the relation between spirit and matter. Eastern Orthodoxy (which Lent ignores) has not been so dualistic. Lent is thus tendentious and sometimes inaccurate in his claims, and we need to examine the evidence afresh to reassess what kind of religion it is. I am going to claim that Christianity is not so near to Platonism as is often supposed, and that properly speaking it is more a religion of unity-in-diversity. I shall try to show this in Part 2 and then spell out the position in much more detail in Parts 3 and 4.

The word "dualism" does not have one simple meaning. In the strong sense, it refers to the world or human beings, that they are flawed in their very nature, over against some pure spiritual state. This is the form of dualism which Lent detects in Platonism and in Christianity. In a weaker sense, it points to the inveterate human tendency to divide some aspect of life into two contrasting or even opposed realms, often for purposes of control. In Part 1, we saw the sharp division into the public and the private realms, with its attendant instability and destructive consequences. Presently we shall meet, for example, the division between individual and society, and between individual citizen and nation state. Such dualisms turn out on inspection to be oversimplifications and distortions. A central issue in this book is the relation of nature and supernature. At the end of Part 2, I shall critique a two-tier view of them and then sketch an integralist approach, which recognizes that there are distinctions to be drawn but affirms a fundamental unity-in-diversity, whose ultimate root lies in God's being and work.

Pythagoras and Plato

Lent tells us that, following the death of Socrates in 399 BC, Plato fled from Athens and travelled far and wide, finding himself specially drawn to Pythagoras' community in south Italy. Pythagoras was not only a geometer. He had noted that the musical note produced by a string is exactly one octave lower than that produced by a string half the length. This was evidence of the essential harmony of nature, and he believed that he could find a mathematical basis for everything, including morality and religion. Pythagoras was also influenced by Orphism, which was a popular cult offering a solution to the problem of death. It claimed each soul was undergoing punishment for a crime it had once committed; the body was described as the tomb of the soul, which would need several lives before it could escape back to its true home. Pythagoras and his followers sought to live out this cosmology in a community life. They adopted quiet contemplation to pursue permanent, rational truth. The soul did not need the body's death for liberation. By relinquishing emotions and bodily desires, a person could achieve release of the soul even while the body was alive.

Plato returned to Athens to found the Academy, which was to last for a thousand years. Lent declares that his philosophy was a fusion of Pythagoras' body–soul dualism, the new concept of pure abstraction, and the mathematical sense of divine order in nature. "By weaving together these different strands of thought, he would create a radically new, comprehensive cosmology that would serve as the underpinning for more than two thousand years of theological, philosophical, and mathematical speculation in the Western world."[2]

Plato: the conflict of body and soul

In the *Republic* (514–21), Plato gives us the allegory of men imprisoned in a deep cave. They face a wall and are chained so that they cannot move their heads. Behind them is a fire, with figures of people and animals moving in front of it. The prisoners can only see shifting shadows on the wall cast by the fire. Because the prisoners have seen nothing else in their lives except these shadows, they think they are seeing reality. Plato explains that our souls are like these prisoners, imprisoned in a world of sense experience, unable to see reality directly, and mistaking these illusory shadows for reality. Plato's metaphors, says Lent, reveal a strong visceral distaste for the body. It is the seat of the appetites or desires, which are in conflict with the mind or reason. Like a charioteer driving unruly horses, reason needs to be in control of these appetites. Lent interestingly points out that Plato's "reason" can be mapped onto what modern neurological scientists call cognitive control, which has been shown to be a crucial function of the prefrontal cortex. In a well-ordered person, says Plato, desire obeys reason, just as in a well-ordered state (set out in the *Republic*) the lower orders obey the rulers. Plato thus has a theory of human consciousness in terms of a conflict between the benevolent force of reasoning and the unruly force of physical desire. In the *Phaedo*, Plato has Socrates saying that the soul can best reflect when it is free of all the distractions such as hearing or sight or pain or pleasure of any kind—that is, when it ignores the body and becomes as far as possible independent in its search for reality. The men in the cave are liberated in stages, first to see the moving figures in the cave, but then brought out of the cave to see the sun, and perceive true reality to be "the pure, the eternal, the immortal, the unchanging". The soul then "ceases its wanderings" and becomes eternal. This is the soul's true nature; it has attained wisdom.[3]

A cascade of dualism

This account of the conflict of body and soul leads into Jeremy Lent's presentation of Plato's worldview. The core is his theory of Forms (Greek *ideai*): for everything that exists in the material world, there exists an ideal form in an immutable world of Ideas. For example, there are many different instances of chairs, but there is only one ideal form of Chair. Similarly there are many ways to be beautiful or good, but there is only one form of Beauty or the Good. Plato's theory of Forms therefore relies on generalization. Identifying true reality requires ignoring particular differences and focussing on what they have in common as a class. It corresponds remarkably well with the rule-making function of the prefrontal cortex. As infants grow, they are primed to detect what is common about a set of experiences and categorize the common factors as abstract concepts with general principles and rules.

Plato believed that when a Form or Idea becomes embodied it gets infected with human flesh. The eternal soul knew all about the immutable world of Ideas before it was incarnated. At birth, it is forced to leave the world of Ideas and become fused with a mortal body, and it forgets most of its previous knowledge. The goal of philosophy is not to learn new truths, but for the soul to rediscover the Truth that was already known prior to its incarnation. Indeed, the very act of thinking about bodily senses is what makes a person mortal, whereas knowledge of eternal Truth is equivalent to attaining immortality. "Here, in Plato's cosmology, is the beginning of the cascade of dualism that would structure the European tradition of thought about the nature of humanity and the universe all the way to the present."[4]

We need to add to Jeremy Lent at this point. Plato saw the arts, particularly painting and poetry, as being at several removes from reality and truth. For they were rooted in the particular and enmeshed in the restless imagination, so were a source more of deception than of truth. When he envisaged his ideal state to match his portrait of the ideal person, with some reluctance he banished the arts from it.[5]

The deification of reason

Plato went on to envisage a creator god who divided up unformed chaos in a mathematical way, creating squares and cubes blended in perfect ratios. So the order of the universe was not intrinsic, but needed a benevolent mathematician-god who imposed rational principles on a primordial mess. The abstract Idea of the Good is therefore the most important thing to learn. It is human reason which connects us with the Good. Man can become divine himself (and in those days such talk was male gendered) by producing in his own nature the order and harmony which the creator originally imposed on the universe. "This is the beginning of the deification of reason that would become a central theme in European thought." The conflict between reason and desire will then be over, and the truly virtuous man will have established complete control over the rest of his consciousness.

Aristotle was one of Plato's early pupils at the Academy. He never accepted Plato's belief in a separate world of Forms, holding rather that they exist only in particulars. But in other respects, he too extolled the divinity of reason. This was also true later of the Stoics: the exercise of reason was necessary for moral perfection, and any passions were merely errors of judgment.[6]

Response to Jeremy Lent (1)

Even though Jeremy Lent's account of Plato is somewhat oversimplified, he is surely right that Plato presents us with a dualistic schema. There is a cosmological dualism which also runs right through every person in the form of a body–soul dualism: even though in this life reason can bring the unruly senses into harmony, there is here a combination of elements which are at odds. As we shall see, it is significant that after Plato this dualism intensified into forms of despair about the prospects for the world and for humanity.

It is, however, important to acknowledge that a doctrine of forms or ideas is not inherently dualistic. As human beings in such a world as this, we cannot live by particulars alone. We have to generalize in order to navigate our way through life. We have to hold in our memories both particulars and generalities in order to find coherence and meaning and function as creatures of time and space.

William R. Crockett has pointed out that though Greek philosophy marks the beginning of rational reflection on myth, in Plato's thought there is an overlap between myth and philosophy:

> Plato is often driven to express some of his deepest philosophical insights in a mythological form ... Symbol, myth, and ritual were the ways in which ancient societies participated in the transcendent or the sacred, the world "behind" or "beyond" the world of ordinary sense-experience ... Genuine knowledge is attained only through participation in the real world that transcends sense-experience ... It is the world of the forms that gives unity and meaning to the world of sense-experience. In Platonism, these two "worlds" are not simply parallel to each other, but the relationship between them is ... one of "participation" ... This means that the image or symbol cannot be thought of apart from the reality in which it participates ... that the relationship between symbol and reality in Platonism is one of unity in distinction.[7]

This notion of participation seems to be both more concrete and more subtle than Jeremy Lent's talk of general rules and general theory in a process of abstraction and is highly relevant to our later discussion of the nature of Christianity, which has perennially been a conversation partner with Platonism and Neoplatonism.

The double task of Christians

Jeremy Lent reminds us that the philosopher Alfred North Whitehead commented famously that the European philosophical tradition "consists in a series of footnotes to Plato".[8] The same may be said of our whole culture. But what of Christianity? The Christian faith has been mediated to us through the Hebrew and the Graeco-Roman civilizations. So an absolutely critical question has been and remains: what blend of Hebrew and Greek elements should prevail? The task of the Christian Church was to be faithful to Christ. There was a massive double task here. One was to see what continuities and discontinuities there were between the Hebrew tradition and the life and teaching of Christ. The other was to keep working out how all that was to relate critically and constructively to the pre-Christian Greek tradition. This task is never finished. I will first see what Lent himself says on the matter, and then respond.

Jeremy Lent: Christ, sin and self-hatred

Jeremy Lent's Chapter 12 on Christianity is entitled: "Sinful Nature: The Dualistic Cosmos of Christianity". He begins by quoting the first words of St John's Gospel: "In the beginning was the Word, and the Word was with God, and the Word was God." The first-century Jewish–Platonist philosopher Philo of Alexandria had spoken of the Word (*Logos*) as a kind of divine architect transforming God's ideas into reality (the Jewish root of this, by the way, is Proverbs 8:22–31). That is, the Word mediates between God's abstract power and the physical world. Now John had the genius to equate Jesus with the *Logos*. Lent then assumes, "This would make Christ a divine figure, an entity apart from normal human existence." So Jesus could transcend his Jewish heritage and become an icon for the entire human race. The idea of God becoming flesh, the Incarnation, would become a central tenet of Christian faith, but Lent claims it is not mentioned anywhere else in the New Testament; rather Jesus had been seen as a human "exalted" by God only at his death. Lent also notes that the Platonists and Neoplatonists had offered salvation only through rigorous intellectual practice; now Christ the Saviour promised a direct connection to eternal salvation for anyone.[9]

As for Paul, Lent sees him as the epitome of a man in inner anguish. Though he spoke of unity in Jesus Christ, and of the overcoming of divisions between Jew and Greek, slave and free, male and female (Galatians 3:28), he was in constant conflict with the apostles and with his converts, and experienced severe struggles within himself. Lent attributes this to his being steeped in the dualistic creeds of his time, known as Gnostic, which were more intense in their negative evaluation of the physical world even than Plato. Paul took these divisions and built a new Christian cosmology upon them. Romans 7 is the classic evidence of this self-loathing. It is a life-and-death struggle between the appetites and the soul. Sexual desire seems to have been his greatest enemy. "His personality, riddled with self-hatred, infused the theology he would bequeath to posterity," and this was "reprised over generations through the inner torment of countless devout Christians".[10]

Response to Jeremy Lent (2)

I wish to counter Jeremy Lent's views with a very different interpretation. In a nutshell, Christianity is not in essence a dualistic religion. It is a religion of unity-in-diversity. I will consider its relation first to the Hebrew tradition and then to the classical Greek.

Paul the Hebrew

Lent makes a double error over the Incarnation. First, he says that evidence for the Incarnation is to be found only in St John's Prologue, and that elsewhere Jesus is a man "exalted" by God at his death. It is true that only John explicitly identifies Jesus Christ with the *Logos*. But Paul has an equivalent passage, where Christ is the image of the invisible God (Colossians 1:15-20) and is identified with the divine wisdom active in creation (Proverbs 8:22-31). Also in Philippians 2:5-11 the one who dies on a cross and is exalted by God and given a name above every name is identical with the one who was in the form of God and emptied himself to be born in human form as a servant or slave.

The second error is that Lent assumes that if Christ were the divine *Logos*, he would be an entity apart from normal human existence. That is exactly what Christians have denied. The Council of Nicaea in 325 decided that Jesus Christ is fully divine, and in 381 the Council of Constantinople went a step further and affirmed the doctrine of the Trinity (Father, Son/*Logos* and Holy Spirit). The Council of Chalcedon in 451 declared Jesus Christ to be wholly divine and wholly human. All these declarations were based on the lived experience of the Church and on the purport of the biblical witness, which included John 3:16–21, Hebrews 1:1–3 and 1 John 4:9. Christianity affirms that finite and infinite did coexist in *and as* the one Person Jesus Christ. I think Lent operates here another dualism: he is prepared to accept anything which passes muster as rational but disqualifies anything purporting to be revelation. Thus he readily says Christianity is monotheistic, but never that it is Trinitarian.

As for Paul, I grant he was a difficult person to live with, and no doubt his theology was influenced by his experience and personality. But we need above all to be accurate about his position. Lent says that Paul was steeped in the dualistic creeds of his time. Paul would certainly know of them in his home city of Tarsus in Asia Minor. But he was a strict Jew, a Pharisee, and it was on that basis that he persecuted the early Christians, before his own Damascus Road conversion. As a Jew he would fully accept that the creation is inherently "very good" (Genesis 1:31—and notice how physical this whole chapter is). He certainly believed that "all have sinned and fall short of the glory of God" (Romans 3:23), and much of the letter to the Romans is taken up with discussing the position of the Jew and the Gentile. The problem for the Jews was that their Law, by defining what was sin, seemed only to increase their propensity to sin.

It is crucial to recognize that there is here no dualism inherent in the very nature of the world or humans: sin is rather a rupture in relationships, primarily with God but involving other humans and nature. The whole Old Testament tells the story of the perverse way in which humans mess up these relationships. But it is at the same time, and primarily, about God. In freely creating the world God chooses to be the God of what is not God, and commits irrevocably to being with us and for us. There is no world or nature in abstraction from God the Creator. God maintains that commitment to fallen humanity, in particular to the people with whom God makes a covenant, constantly seeking the restoration of relations. Israel persistently jeopardizes that covenant. The hope is born that this perverse propensity to sin will finally be overcome.

What Paul declared is that God through Jesus Christ brought about reconciliation as a free gift. It was not just an offer which it was then entirely up to us to accept or refuse. God had actually by Christ's ministry, death and resurrection created a new covenant relationship, and the people of God had been reconstituted in the form of the Church, the body of Christ. Paul knew this was a decisive and final act. He had a firm grasp of what we call eschatology. The Jews had long believed there would be a final reckoning of God with humanity in a last judgment. The Christian belief was that this final act, both of judgment and reconciliation, had taken place in Christ in the midst of history. There was therefore a great urgency to persuade not only the Jews but the whole human race to respond to this decisive act, by calling them into the new covenant community. The ultimate vision of Paul (evident in Ephesians) is of all people and indeed all things being brought into a final unity-in-diversity in Christ, when God would be all in all. Hence his numerous missionary journeys criss-crossing the Mediterranean world.

Lent is therefore absolutely right to point out that Paul preached that in Christ all were being drawn into a unity as children of God, and his words at Galatians 3:28 on Jew and Gentile, slave and free, men and women show the overcoming of the deepest divisions in the world of his day (which are conspicuously still with us). It is worth remembering that this preaching was bound to be a perpetual reminder to him of how he had persecuted the Church (1 Corinthians 15:9; Galatians 1:13). In his first letter to the Corinthians, he was distraught to discover that the Christian community had fallen into factions and were even at odds when they broke bread: "When you meet together, it is not the Lord's Supper that you eat" (1 Corinthians 11:20). They needed to "discern the body"—whether of Christ in the bread, or of Christ in the body of believers. In Romans 7, he is presumably writing of himself not before his conversion, but as the Christian he now is. Even he cannot avoid still sinning, thus undermining the credibility of the very gospel which he has been commissioned by God to preach. But he ends the chapter by thanking God through Christ that he will be delivered.

Over the terms he uses, Paul is typically rather imprecise. He clearly believed in what was later called the Incarnation, in line with his positive view of the physical creation: Jesus Christ was indeed born in the flesh. But he also uses "flesh" in a negative sense, which is most apparent when he criticizes living "according to the flesh", where he clearly means trying to live in your own strength, without regard for God (Romans 8:1–11). It is also worth noting that the sins of the flesh include idolatry, sorcery, enmity, strife, jealousy, anger, dissension, party spirit and envy, all of which clearly engulf the mind, even if some material thing may be the occasion for them (Galatians 5:19–21). In Romans 12:1–2, Paul urges Christians to "present your bodies as a living sacrifice" and not to "be conformed to this world, but be transformed by the renewal of your mind" (cf. Ephesians 4:22–4). The goal of redemption is the restoration of the person to integrity or wholeness, which is inseparable from the restoration of society and all things.

Classical Greek religion and culture

Jeremy Lent is entirely right to say that the Christian faith was offered to all, and not to an elite. And masses of people lived by the age-old Greek religion and culture. The vitality and achievements of classical Greek civilization captivated the Romans and have continued to captivate the Western world. The key seems to lie in their understanding of the place of human beings in relation to this world and to the gods. The Greeks had no sense of a richer life in the hereafter and lived this life with great intensity. C. M. Bowra wrote *The Greek Experience* after a lifetime of study. He says that "the Greek sense of the holy was based much less on a feeling of the goodness of the gods than on a devout respect for their incorruptible beauty and unfailing strength . . . It gave to men an increased self-respect because they resembled them. It was good to possess, even in the humblest degree, qualities shared with the gods", and they took delight and pride in any unusual manifestation of these powers. Bowra illustrates this from Pindar (518–438 BC), who wrote lyric odes to the victors in the various games, and understood the Greek religious temperament from the inside:

> Single is the race, single
> Of men and of gods;
> From a single mother we both draw breath.
> But a difference of power in everything
> Keeps us apart;
> For the one is as nothing, but the brazen sky
> Stays a fixed habitation for ever.
> Yet we can in greatness of mind

Or of body be like the Immortals,
Though we know not to what goal
By day or in the nights
Fate has written that we shall run.[11]

This kinship yet difference in power created a tension in which the Greeks could flourish culturally.[12] Of course it was polytheistic, with a plethora of forces at work in the world. Its pantheon was a projection of the best and the worst in human beings. But at least it was personal. The symbols and myths of ancient Greece have a vitality which is lacking in Platonism. It is very important to realize that for centuries ordinary folk really did feel a vivid connection with the gods. The few surviving fragments of Sappho, for instance, testify to the warmth and affection which they felt for them, and the delight and joy they found in life. In their tragedies, notably in Aeschylus' trilogy the *Oresteia*, they felt their way towards some kind of unifying and just force behind all the multiplicity and division in the world, and this was done not in an abstracting way but by deeper reflection on concrete experience.

As David Jenkins argued in his very perceptive book *The Glory of Man*, by the time of Christ much of this vitality, fostered in the small city states of Greece, had been eroded in the vastness of the Roman empire and the unpredictable fortunes of its populations. This was reflected in the growing popularity of Gnostic sects which fervently proclaimed that the body was indeed a tomb, despaired of this world, and by their rituals enabled the soul to escape from it back to its true home. There is a real sense that Christianity restored hope to the world and encouraged a more positive engagement with it. It taught that "matter matters", not by wordy argument, but by worshipping a God who was transcendent yet also at every point irrevocably with and for the created world in an earthly and earthy way. God had created humans in God's image. And God had in the Incarnation of the Son united heaven and earth in Christ and was drawing all its diversity into a unity in him.

Plato and Christianity

It is therefore time to clarify the relationship of Platonism and Christianity. It is not nearly so close as is often supposed.

It is perfectly intelligible that the early Christians took up the unity-in-distinction they found in Plato's doctrine of Forms or Ideas. As we shall see in Part 3, their understanding of the Liturgy was saturated with the notion that symbols participate in the reality they signify, and so render it present. And this was interwoven with the biblical sense of types and figures which reflect God's unwavering dynamic action in the history of salvation.

Though the Fathers of the early Church were not agreed on how far Platonic philosophy was compatible with Christian faith, they were all profoundly influenced by it, and interrelated theology and philosophy. Their primary concern tended to be for their immortal soul and its relation to eternity. They moved inwards to a life of self-knowledge, to seek greater inner purity through self-mastery and self-control, and prioritized the pursuit of virtue, contemplation and solitude. So there developed a certain kind of Christian ascetic spirituality.[13]

There is no doubt at all that the practice of the Christian faith requires *askesis* (disciplined living). Devotion to God is a prime virtue and it needs to be constantly cultivated. This runs right through the experience of ancient Israel and is evident throughout the New Testament, in the life of John the Baptist and Jesus Christ himself, and as a constant demand placed upon Christians. But if Platonism becomes dominant, it can lead to a powerful dualism, as is evident, for example, in the lifestyle and thought of Origen (185–249). It can threaten the Hebrew conviction that the created material world is "very good", and remains so, whatever the distortions introduced by human sin. It is not inherently evil but has its place in the purposes of God. This is supremely endorsed in the Incarnation of Jesus Christ. At a time of great controversy over the humanity of Christ, the Cappadocian Father Gregory Nazianzen (d. 390) affirmed that what Christ had not assumed, he had not healed: he had to be fully human, including mind and body, if redemption was to be effective for humankind. This is a great bulwark against dualism.

Another Cappadocian Father pioneered a form of ascetic monastic community which was urban and devoted to the care of the poor and the sick. Basil (c.330–379) became bishop of Caesarea in Cappadocia (eastern Turkey). It had a pretty harsh climate and terrain, and after the failure of the harvest caused widespread starvation, Basil not only called for communal sharing, as in the early Church, and condemned exploitative moneylenders, but also set up and developed a complex of buildings which served as hospital for the sick, shelter for the poor, and feeding station for the starving. He lived there and personally washed the feet of the poor and distributed food. He ploughed into it much of his own resources and received grants from the emperor. This became a model for a form of socially concerned monasticism in later centuries, East and West.[14]

Since those days there have been transformations in our understanding which have brought out the importance of this earthly life much more. Thomas Aquinas broke with centuries of Platonic dominance and explored the Christian faith using the philosophy of Aristotle, who had rejected the ideal world of forms, holding that they exist only in particulars, and who pursued biology, how creatures grow in time and space to maturity. This contributed to a deeper recognition of empirical studies though sense-experience, and from the seventeenth century to the rise of modern science and medicine. Furthermore, this was bound up with an increasing recognition of the potential of earthly human relationships, shown in the determination to improve the conditions of this life, and with the rise of democracies, where people assume responsibility for their wellbeing and set up the necessary institutions for their developing cultures. This opened up new areas for Christian responsibility. Gregory's great affirmation turns out to carry within it the call to Christians to collaborate with other citizens in the continual scrutiny of our culture and the operation of power within it.

In pursuing this rebalancing towards a more Hebraic outlook, we can draw out some of the contrasts between Platonism and Christianity, which are essentially a rejection of Platonic dualism.

Whereas Plato tells a story to illustrate a more abstract and general truth, Christianity is fundamentally the story of what God has done, and all abstractions and generalizations are secondary.

Whereas Platonic cosmology envisages the supreme being in mathematical terms, imposing order on a recalcitrant chaos, Christianity speaks of an ultimate unity-in-diversity of Persons, the Trinity, which freely creates all that is. There is no cosmological dualism.

Whereas in Plato the soul is immortal and rational, and the body is temporal and an obstruction to knowledge, in the Christian schema the starting point is the unity of the person, within which diverse capacities, spirit, soul, mind and body, are present. There is no immortal "thing" in a physical "thing".

Whereas in the Platonic scheme of redemption the immortal soul has to overcome the unruly appetites and desires by rational means in order to escape this corrupt world, the Christian recognizes that no part is untouched by sin, and humans cannot forge their own redemption. I am reminded of William Temple's discussion of moral evil in *Nature, Man and God* back in 1932–4:

> It cannot be accounted for by reference to the survival of animal impulses into the rational stage of development. The centre of the trouble is not the turbulent appetites, though they are troublesome enough, and the human faculty for imagination increases their turbulence. But the centre of the trouble is the personality as a whole, which is self-centred and can only be wholesome and healthy if it is God-centred. This whole personality in action is the will; and it is the will which is perverted. It is the form taken by our knowledge of good and evil that perverts our nature. We know good and evil, but know them amiss. We take them into our lives, but we mis-take them. The corruption is at the centre of our rational and purposive life... *We totally misconceive alike the philosophic and the practical problem of evil if we picture it as the winning of control over lawless and therefore evil passions by a righteous but insufficiently powerful reason or spirit. It is the spirit which is evil; it is reason which is perverted; it is aspiration itself which is corrupt.*

So we live with two foci: God and self. For our integration we must affirm that the real centre of the real world is God. The colossal structures of enlightened egoism will never effect deliverance from self-centredness. "Such radical conversion must be an act of God. It cannot be a process only of enlightenment. Nothing can suffice but a redemptive act."[15]

The Christian claim is that God has graciously taken the initiative in Christ fully to restore our humanity. It is the restoration of access to God in our primary relationship and also a restoration of relationship with the rest of humanity and the natural world. Indeed it is more than restoration. The redemptive act of God is fundamentally creative—a new and final chapter in creation, and anyone in Christ is a new creation (cf. 2 Corinthians 5:16–21). The goal is the unity-in-diversity of all (cf. especially Ephesians 1:3–10).

Knowledge therefore is not, as in Plato, a recovery of what the soul already once knew. Through the Holy Spirit, God's creative act brings new knowledge and inspires humans to be adventurous and creative in their new life. (The Parable of the Prodigal Son in Luke 15:11–32 demonstrates this—see the address in Appendix 1 of this book.)

Thus the Christian schema is *personal and relational* from start to finish. Moreover, redemption is not just that of the soul or mind. It is the redemption of all people and all things—of all that Christ took on in his Incarnation. At every point, the Christian faith holds us to the *physical nature of the cosmos and ourselves within it*. To say that humans are in the image of God is not to single out reason and mind as the connecting point. The image is best considered to be our capacity to live in relationship, with God and with other humans and nature. This scenario keeps firmly in view both the glory and the limits inherent in human life. It treats our bodily nature as a gift from God and checks our ambition to cut loose from living with others and bearing responsibility for them.

This position warrants us locating our sexuality non-dualistically within a complementary and equal relationship with another person—a basic human unity-in-diversity. It is a defect of the story in Genesis 3 that it is the woman who is tempted by the serpent and she then tempts her husband. It is important to bear in mind that the story was shaped and passed down by men, and it bears their stamp. No woman would have written the story that way! Consider the prevailing Victorian view (still with us) of the relations between women and men. The Brontë sisters felt the impact acutely, and all produced novels of a high order which reflect their experience. Anne in *The Tenant of Wildfell Hall* writes very directly (no doubt from personal experience of dealing with her brother Branwell) about Helen, trapped in a dreadful marriage and with a child, and eventually summoning the courage to leave it. Charlotte exposes both Brocklehurst and St John Rivers as chilling representatives of Christianity, each in their own way, and Jane Eyre repeatedly shows up the inferior status of women. She longs for freedom to shape her own life, and right from childhood has the feistiness to call out hypocrisy and injustice. Not for her the self-suppression of a Rivers. She seeks not some ethereal Christianity but earthly happiness. Having humbled and restored Rochester, after ten years of marriage she tells us of their perfect union of "flesh of my flesh and bone of my bone": she experiences in this life the restoration of paradise (Genesis 2:23). By contrast, much of Victorian Christianity passively sanctified our fallen state, such as men ruling women (Genesis 3:16), as if it was decreed by God, thus nullifying the purpose of Christ's work in and for the world. It is deeply tragic that so many in later generations misinterpreted Paul and fell into a pathological dualism.

I now resume Jeremy Lent's account, focussing on the way Christianity became an incubator for scientific thought, which in turn shaped our modern vision of the conquest of nature.

Jeremy Lent: Descartes and the Scientific Revolution

In the Introduction and Part 1, I mentioned Descartes as one of the instigators of the Enlightenment. Jeremy Lent tells us that he experienced a vision of an angel telling him that mathematics was the key to unlocking the secrets of the universe. From then on, he trusted only his intellect. He determined not to rely on any previous opinions, even his own senses. "I shall now close my eyes, stop up my ears, turn away all my senses, even efface from my thought all images of corporeal things, or at least ... I shall consider them as being vain and false; ... thus communing only with myself, and examining my inner self..." Out of this kind of exercise came the dictum *Cogito ergo sum*—"I think, therefore I am." "I thereby concluded that I was a substance, of which the whole essence or nature consists in thinking, and which ... needs no place and depends on no material thing."[16] The irony is that he was really building his ideas on the same dualistic underpinning as Plato two thousand years before him.

He went on to say that "the mind, by which I am what I am, is entirely distinct from my body".[17] He became wary of using the term "soul", since it was ambiguous. It offended against the notion of precise and distinct ideas. In the Enlightenment, the soul became more and more problematical and was left to the theologians, and mind became the ubiquitous term in Western thought.

A corollary to all this, which Descartes himself saw perfectly clearly, was that if our bodies are mere matter, then so is nature, since no other entity possesses a mind capable of reason. He did not recognize any difference between machines made by craftsmen and natural bodies. So Descartes eliminated any intrinsic value from the natural world. With nothing sacred about nature, it became available for the human intellect to use remorselessly for its own purposes. Every aspect of the natural world was fair game for inquiry, investigation and exploitation.

Lent points out that the Protestant movement put its own unique stamp on the split between reason and emotion by emphasizing the importance of cognitive control as proof of God's favour. The Puritans believed that the natural state of humanity was impulsive and untamed; those who were successful in restraining their passions demonstrated that they were God's chosen, predestined for heaven. "This formed the foundation of the Protestant ethic, which created the moral underpinning for modern American society with its emphasis on systematic rationalisation and goal orientation."[18] I would rather say it was one important contributory factor to that moral underpinning. Readers can find a fascinating British instance of this ethic in Madeleine Bunting's portrait of Lord Leverhulme in *Love of Country: A Hebridean Journey*, pp. 238–60.

Response to Jeremy Lent (3)

First, it has to be said that Descartes did not prove his *Cogito ergo sum*. What he actually proved was just that there is thought. Only by a wild leap could one call a thought "I". Of course this made sense to him because he absolutized reason and mind. He was indeed re-presenting the Platonic view, substituting "mind" for "soul", thus reinforcing its dualism.

The incoherence of this dualism can be exposed by asking whether I am a soul with a body, or a body with a soul. We are certainly a compound of at least two facets, but to suppose we are really made up of two disparate "things" suggests that whenever we act there is a double process going on of the mental and the physical. This seems at variance with our assumption that we are a single person and is a recipe for the pathologies which Lent portrays.

Today there really is no excuse for a dualistic view of human beings. The modern scientific worldview is succinctly set out by Arthur R. Peacocke. Nature is enormously complex and varied, basically relational, consisting of a hierarchy of levels of organization, from the micro-world of the sub-atomic, through the macro-world of the biosphere, to the mega-world of the galaxies, immense in distance and time. The whole is dynamic, always in process, a nexus of evolving forms, essentially incomplete, inexhaustible in its potential for change and open to the future.[19] Within it our human capacities have developed over millions of years, along with all other creatures. There has been a process of emergence of new and higher capacities, but never at the expense of our physical nature. Indeed the physical reveals its full potential when it is indwelt by the higher levels of life, where mind can hold together a succession of events in memory, and humans can build up enduring cultures. We are ourselves a unity-in-diversity.

As Jeremy Lent rightly pointed out, the natural environment has been treated as open to exploitation by humans with their "god-like" faculty of reason. Christians have of course justifiably replied that this is a misunderstanding of "dominion" (Genesis 1:26), but not consistently followed that through. They now do their bit for the environment at an individual level, but most do not go deeply into the ramifications. One is the matter of land ownership. Madeleine Bunting, in her *Love of Country: A Hebridean Journey*, writes that "Rum tells a stark story of how land was once used, how it became a commodity demonstrating status, and finally how its emptiness was romanticized as wilderness. Nowhere in Scotland encapsulates more succinctly these transitions and the impact of the English innovation of individual landownership, which had repercussions around the world under the British Empire." Bunting observes that the Clearances resonate powerfully, because they are a history repeated in many places around the world, where preindustrial communal cultures have come into contact with capitalism, and the result has been bitter conflicts:

> They can be traced back to two radical innovations in land rights. The first was that land could be a commodity owned by one individual. In clan society . . . that a piece of land could be owned like a horse or pot was not just inconceivable: it was a denial of the ties of relationship which bound people together. The anonymity and instrumentalism of a market economy in which land and people could be routinely used and exploited within a cash system proved to be deeply traumatic: it resulted not just in loss of access to the land, but also in a loss of self-understanding.

The second innovation came from the Puritans, especially in North America. They advanced

> a right to land which they deemed to be "vacant". Any land use which was not one of intensive human industry met the definition of vacant. In support of their claim, they quoted Biblical verses requiring that the land be fruitful. This was to have huge implications in the dispossession of Native Americans . . . and these ideas flowed back to Scotland. Land had to be productive, and that meant it had to generate a monetary surplus; this was ordained by God.[20]

This God was of course uncannily like the energetic and well-organized Puritans themselves.

It was no accident that Descartes gave dualism a new twist. In various ways, dualism had become more and more entrenched in Church and society over a thousand years. Augustine (354–430) was an influential and ambivalent figure. He had a remarkably fertile mind, which profoundly influenced both Catholicism and Protestantism. On the positive side, standing right at the end of the classical period, he firmly upheld the view that symbols participate in the reality they point to, and, like Paul, he believed that participation in the Eucharist meant participation both in Christ himself and in his body the Church (the importance of this will become clearer in Part 3). He also trenchantly defended the view that salvation is from start to finish solely the work of God's grace. But he marred his work by speculation. Through a mistranslation of a clause in Paul's Letter to the Romans, Augustine interpreted Adam's sin as incurring guilt for evermore on the whole human race and conceived the transmission as pollution, particularly by the sex act. This fed into a gloomy view which, though never the official one, was very influential in later centuries. At the start is a God who punishes Adam for a monstrous original sin. At Calvary, Christ pleads with the Father, making a propitiatory sacrifice. It readily suggests a wrathful transcendent deity, anxious for his honour and majesty, being placated by a plaintive human Son fending off our punishment. Life becomes a grim struggle to avoid the final punishment of hell fire. This undermines the Johannine sense that God so loved the whole world as to send his Son to save it. Salvation is rather the privilege of some individual souls in the life beyond. Augustine's views seriously affected our ideas of how we are to live in this life, importing a fearfulness, particularly over our sexuality, and how we bring up children. It is a travesty of the gospel, as it seems to open up a split within God between wrath and love, Father and Son. It is a relief to turn to Paul: "If God is for us, who is against us?" Nothing "will be able to separate us from the love of God in Christ Jesus our Lord" (Romans 8:31–9).

Dualisms within the Church of England

There are persistent forms of dualism within the Church of England. *The Book of Common Prayer* heavily emphasizes the penitential element carried over from the mediaeval period and reinforced by the Reformation with its strong accent on sin and moral exhortation. Urged in Morning and Evening Prayer to acknowledge and confess our manifold sins and wickedness, the congregation declares, "There is no health in us". This is really to abstract our nature from its setting within the supernatural, or to put it more dynamically and personally, the constant working of God's grace within us. It appears to make redemption something external to us and ineffectual within us, as if it has for ever to begin anew. The assurance that "we are very members incorporate in the mystical body of thy Son, which is the blessed company of all faithful people" does occur late in the Communion service, but only in an optional prayer.

The weaker form of dualism became evident in the outworking of the idea of establishment: a single nation with two realms of religion and state. When it was originally created by the declaration of Royal Supremacy by Henry VIII and cemented by Queen Elizabeth I, the two realms were virtually inseparable, since the need was to secure national unity in an age of dire religious and political conflict. Elizabeth was continually threatened by foreign invasion, and her ministers were paranoid about insurrection from within. *The Book of Common Prayer* was a potent way of imposing unity. But the effect was that the monarch through Parliament controlled the Church of England for 400 years. The Royal Supremacy solidified a hierarchical society and paralysed any serious social reform or questioning of British conduct in the public arena. In the course of time, the view gained ground that religion was primarily concerned with the individual soul, whilst the public realm was governed by law. There is a similar pattern in the settlements in the plethora of Protestant states in Germany during the Reformation, with the emergence of the "doctrine of the two kingdoms" (God's kingdom and the political realm), which had a hugely inhibiting effect on the Germans offering timely and effective resistance to Hitler.

This growing dualism between religion and politics was a very handy tool to let necessity triumph in the public realm. A good example is to be found in Nicholas Rogers' *Murder on the Middle Passage: The Trial of Captain Kimber*, which is a thorough investigation of Kimber's trial in 1792 for the murder of a teenage slave girl and well shows the sheer complexity of the detail. The abolitionists had made some headway among the public in exposing the horrors of slavery. But the slave traders passionately wanted to exclude sentiment from the public realm. Having once built up the slave trade, the British were trapped in the supposed necessity of keeping it going for commercial, political and strategic reasons. It was not as if natural law or humanitarianism was unknown. One of the greatest abolitionists was Granville Sharp, who campaigned against any toleration of slavery in Britain. He invested decades of his life in a legal crusade on behalf of the enslaved. In 1769, he wrote to the Lord High Chancellor, asking him to take note of an advertisement for the sale of a slave as a "notorious breach of the laws of nature, humanity and equity". It was he who gave full support to the Sierra Leone Settlement Scheme for black people from Britain and later from Nova Scotia.[21] Yet a strong view of what was due to a human being as such had little traction. In fact, the Kimber case, it seems, is one of the first where the charge of murder of a slave was even allowed; before that, slaves were primarily cargo! (See the dedication of this book.)

An excellent example of Establishment Christianity is to be found in Margaret Thatcher's speech to the General Assembly of the Church of Scotland on 21 May 1988.[22] It is important to grasp first that it is strikingly free from being technocratic–emotivist. She declares, "The truths of the Judaic-Christian tradition are infinitely precious, not only ... because they are true, but also because they provide the moral impetus which alone can lead to that peace, in the true meaning of the word, for which we all long." She denies that spiritual redemption and social reform are quite separate and speaks at length of the relevance of Christianity to public policy. "The Christian religion ... is a fundamental part of our national heritage ... Indeed we are a nation whose ideals are founded on the Bible." The Old Testament gives us the Ten Commandments, the injunction to love our neighbour, and a strict code of law. The New Testament records the Incarnation, the teachings of Christ, the establishment of the Kingdom of God, and a re-emphasis on loving our neighbour as ourselves and "Do-as-you-would-be-done-by". From these key elements, we gain a view of the universe, a proper attitude to work, and the principles to shape economic and social life. She takes account of the huge changes between biblical times and modernity, with its vastly increased complexity. "In our generation, the only way we can ensure that no one is left without sustenance, help or opportunity, is to have laws to provide for health and education, pensions for the elderly, succour for the sick and disabled." She expects disagreements over what kind of political and social institutions and laws we should have and looks for courtesy and mutual respect in working through them.

Mrs Thatcher plainly expects that those who are not Christians will also recognize and accept their responsibilities. She is an enthusiast for democracy, and in a thoroughly non-emotivist way: it is not a matter simply of counting heads to discover what the majority want. No majority can take away God-given rights. Democracy most effectively safeguards the value of the individual, and, more than any other system, restrains the abuse of power by the few. "But there is little hope for democracy if the hearts of men and women in democratic societies cannot be touched by a call to something greater than themselves. Political structures, state institutions, collective ideals—these are not enough ... The politician's role is a humble one." For her, the foundations need to be Christian, and you cannot take the fruits of Christianity unless you nurture the roots. So Christianity and the state have complementary roles.

Mrs Thatcher also praises tolerance as one of the great principles of the Judaic-Christian inheritance:

> People with other faiths and cultures have always been welcomed in our land, assured of equality under the law, of proper respect and open friendship. There is absolutely nothing incompatible between this and our desire to maintain the essence of our own identity. There is no place for racial or religious intolerance in our creed.

Much of this is well said. There is a content and an integrity here which actually poses a challenge to her current professed heirs and successors and their ideology. But there are also very serious flaws in Mrs Thatcher's understanding of the world and of Christianity. She moves almost entirely between two poles: individual citizen and nation-state. The heavy emphasis on individuals and their responsibilities is clear:

> Any set of social and economic arrangements which is not founded on the acceptance of individual responsibility will do nothing but harm ... Intervention by the State must never become so great that it effectively removes personal responsibility.

Nobody of course should deny or remove individual responsibility. But this way of putting it invites an odious moralism: the "deserving rich" spotting fecklessness in others and legislating accordingly. This is made all the more likely because there is a gaping hole here, which is not an oversight but an integral part of her ideology. One recalls her famous dictum that there is no such thing as society, only individuals and their families. This is a distorting dualism of individual/society. In reality, we are also inherently social and communal creatures, with natural bonds of solidarity, and are interdependent for our flourishing. In traditional thought, politics, whether local or national, arises out of the pre-existent life of society and its numerous natural associations, and is there to promote a common good which entails the good of each of its members. This requires us to take account of the forces operative in society and impacting for good or ill on individuals and their families. The Judaeo-Christian religion is patently rooted first in the life of the Israelite community, where each member counts within it and there should be no poor; and Jesus Christ does not preach individualism but refounds the people of Israel in the form of the community of the Church, from the local to the international, where if one member suffers, all suffer.

This flaw shows up also in Mrs Thatcher's heavy emphasis on freedom to choose. "From the beginning man has been endowed with the right to choose between good and evil." The story actually has nothing to do with a right to choose, or a clear and simple distinction between good and evil. It is primarily about our journey in this world, each one of us, from innocence to maturity and wisdom. We noted earlier from William Temple that the issue is whether we are God-centred or self-centred. We know good and evil amiss. This does not mean that we are all plain wicked. For us to be trapped in self-centredness, it only requires us to be no better than we are. There is indeed a solidarity in bondage to sin across the whole human race, which cannot be handled in individualistic terms by appeal to human rights and human will and thought.

Mrs Thatcher goes on to say that we were made in God's image and "are expected to use all our power of thought and judgment in exercising that choice ... if we open our hearts to God, he has promised to work within us". There is an intense focus in Mrs Thatcher's speech on the performance of our moral duties. It includes a great stress on hard work, and on the accumulation of wealth. She is right to say that it is not the creation of wealth that is wrong but the love of money for its own sake, but it is striking that wealth is seen predominantly as money, and sure enough entrepreneurs came to be hailed as *the* wealth creators. There is no sense of the workforce being co-creators, even less of other forms of wealth, such as our relationships with one another in society and with nature, or of cultural goods like appreciation of the arts and sciences. It is a very narrow activism, with little room for leisure to appreciate life. In specifically Christian terms, she comes nowhere near the centrality of celebrating what God has done and is doing, from creation itself and the gift of all of us to the fuller appreciation of God's supreme self-giving presence in the Incarnation, life, death and resurrection of Christ.

This aggressive activism seems to flow from a negative and pessimistic view of persons and the world. Life is an unending fight against the threats of competitors and enemies, whether foreigners or home-grown. There is no readiness for an imaginative grasp of people who have a different cultural experience. It is really no surprise that at the end Mrs Thatcher produces another dualism: this life and the next. She speaks glowingly of the hymn "I vow to thee my country". "It begins with a triumphant assertion of what might be described as secular patriotism, a noble thing indeed in a country like ours: 'I vow to thee my country all earthly things above; entire, whole and perfect the service of my love.'" As we know, it is a love that asks no question, that pays the price. She then goes on to that other "country I heard of long ago", where "soul by soul and silently her shining bounds increase". As we shall see in the rest of this book, her account falls far short of a Christian understanding of the drawing of all people and all things into a unity-in-diversity rooted in the Trinitarian God.

There is an irony here. Mrs Thatcher was by conviction opposed to technocracy-emotivism, but she welcomed Hayekian views, and her account of the world and the faith proved too deeply flawed to stem the tide of his ideology.

Surveying our journey so far

Jeremy Lent is justified in seeing a marked tendency towards dualism of various kinds in the Christian tradition. He is right to claim that such a view of Christianity would disable it from grappling effectively with our cultural predicament. I have, however, tried to show that this is not a satisfactory account of Christianity. Certainly, as I argued by reference to William Temple, there can be no glossing over the gravity of human sin: humans cannot forge their own redemption. But sin is not a sign of an inherent dualism: it is rather a rupture of relationships, and the Christian faith is primarily about the power of God to overcome that rupture. It tells of a God who creates the world out of love and sustains it in love, even when humans act perversely. God decisively acts in Christ to inaugurate a new and final era. God reconstitutes the people of Israel as the Church, the body of Christ, and calls all people to belong to that body. This is an eschatological process. On the one hand the redemptive work of God in Christ is already operative throughout the created order in the here and now; on the other hand, it is incomplete, but there remains the promise of an ultimate resolution into a perfected unity-in-diversity in God. This is not just the salvation of individual souls but embraces the whole of creation. To quote Temple again, "No object is sufficient for the love of God short of *the world* itself."[23]

Our journey over the first two parts of this work is complete. I started out in Part 1 from the division and fragmentation endemic in our country and the world at large. I have been on a quest for sources of coherence and meaning, so that each human being in society can contribute towards a shared common life, conscious of a fuller, if elusive, integrity or wholeness. I found many clues, for example, in the work of Daniel Barenboim and Edward Said.

I rejected the pursuit of the Holy Grail of impersonal knowledge, the dividing of life into atomic bits of information, and the view of science as the amassing of atomic facts. I followed Michael Polanyi in insisting on the personal character of our knowing and pointed up the dangers of an unfettered technology destructive of persons.

Even when set in a personal context, science and technology are still inadequate to sustain our culture. Their rationality needs to be complemented by other forms of rationality, visible in the arts, ethics and religion, which are equally forms of public knowledge. We need to know who we are as persons, and how we are to relate fully to the social and natural worlds in which we are embedded. So we read Alasdair MacIntyre's words, "I am my body and my body is social, born to those parents in this community with a specific social identity." This led into the idea of a practice, covering a wide range of activities, coherent and socially established, with goods internal to them and virtues cultivated to achieve standards of excellence. The whole enterprise of building and sustaining a culture is itself a multiple practice. At every turn, it is a personal endeavour, and we have to give primacy to persons, and defend them against loss.

Finally in Part 1, I noted the importance of symbols. We live a shared life in communities, and they change within a changing world across time. All our knowing takes place within time. The whole human system of knowing is a spiral of self-extending symbolic activity, not so much the labelling of objects as the re-enacting of a performance. For reality turns out to be a mobile, dynamic pattern whose best analogy is not mechanical but musical (Pythagoras was right here). The whole has an open texture which allows for inexhaustible creativity and gratuitous excess. For persons have generative and creative capacities, which respond to the generative and creative capacities of the universe itself.

The question arises whether these capacities find their source in a Creator who is not only "beyond" the universe and generative of it but also present within it. No proof as the conclusion of an argument is possible. But one can at least experiment with the idea that the whole process of cultural activity could be related to such a "Person", as a gathering point of coherence and meaning, who provided ultimate sense. That "Person" would be both transcendent over the world process and immanent within it: not simply generative of it but intimately involved in the growth of the human spiral of knowing from the very beginning. The human spirit would, as it were, be aligned with the divine creative Spirit. The question arises whether there are forms of Christianity which would endorse and underpin that approach.

There are at least two strands in the Anglican tradition which would be supportive of this approach. Both start out from a Trinitarian position: God the Father, the source and end of creation, has acted decisively in Jesus Christ to renew all things in the Son through the Holy Spirit. Christians as members of Christ's body, the Church, respond by the continual practice of worship, reflection and action in the world. The first strand is the dialogic way of William Temple and his successors, which I set out in *Anglican Social Theology* (2014), edited by Malcolm Brown, in the chapter "The Temple Tradition". The other is an integralist approach, sketched by John Hughes in the same volume in "After Temple? The Recent Renewal of Anglican Social Thought". I wish now briefly to show its character. Parts 3 and 4 will spell it out in much more detail.

An integralist approach

The roots of this approach lie in the Church of the first five centuries, but its developers were Roman Catholics of the twentieth century, of whom the most prominent was Henri de Lubac (1896–1991). He was French, a Jesuit and a teacher of theology, who immersed himself in the tradition, particularly Thomas Aquinas, Augustine and the Greek Fathers of the early Church. He came to realize that the version of Thomism which was officially endorsed by the Roman Catholic Church was not faithful to Thomas himself. For it had introduced a sharp division between the natural and supernatural realms, where the natural appeared as self-contained and autonomous. When in 1950 Pope Pius XII produced his encyclical *Humani Generis*, de Lubac's interpretation of Thomas led to him being suspended from his teaching and virtually ostracized. However, he was well supported by other eminent theologians, and after Pius died in 1958, he was invited by Pope John XXIII to act as consultant in the preparations for the Second Vatican Council (1962–5), and he played a prominent role during and long after the Council.

De Lubac saw that there was in fact a whole range of issues on which the Church had become narrow and rigid, with immensely destructive consequences. The separation between the natural and supernatural, he believed, was a sign that since mediaeval times the tradition had become too rationalistic, often substituting a philosophical schema for the living God, and taking refuge in the safety of propositions, instead of being interested in the truth which the propositions could only partially formulate. It had virtually given up on the symbolic thinking characteristic of antiquity and the early Church, whereby the symbol participates in the reality to which it points. Moreover, the legacy of Roman law had led to the Church itself being seen primarily as a juridical institution whose chief task was to guide individual souls to salvation. On the one hand, the Vatican had entered into alliances with dictators (notoriously there were concordats with Hitler and Mussolini, and the Roman Church backed Franco in Spain), and on the other hand the Church had fallen into individualism (for example, by preaching almsgiving to the exclusion of social justice). De Lubac believed this persistent tendency had led to modern humanists being predominantly anti-theistic; if the Church had been more faithful to the tradition, perhaps the error of Marxism-Leninism would never have arisen or spread so disastrously.

De Lubac realized that Thomas Aquinas had deep roots in Augustine and the early Church Fathers. He reflected on Augustine's famous dictum, "Thou hast made us for thyself, and our heart is restless until it finds its rest in thee." Human beings in their innermost nature are oriented to a goal which is beyond themselves; they cannot be fully satisfied by anything purely natural or inner-worldly. Yet it is a goal they cannot reach in their own strength: their fundamental longing can only be fulfilled by the gift of grace from God. How are we to envisage this?

De Lubac reflected critically on the very terminology "nature" and "supernature". In distinguishing them sharply, Pius XII in *Humani Generis* had the laudable intention of safeguarding the integrity of each. But how then were they to be related, particularly as supernature is evidently not on the same plane as nature? The relation would be only extrinsic, in which case the supernatural could easily be envisaged as the decree of an arbitrary God to be mediated by the power structure of an authoritarian church.

This becomes even clearer if we switch from philosophical language to thinking in personal terms: the living God in relation to human beings. God created all that is not God *gratuitously*, that is, as pure gift. This is radical creation *ex nihilo*: there is no preceding recipient on whom the gift is conferred; all things and all persons are themselves gift. God's fundamental intention in creation is to communicate God's own self as absolute love, so that human beings recognize the call of God to love, and desire to know the giver more fully and to receive more of the mysterious gift.

It is very important to grasp, with Thomas Aquinas and Henri de Lubac, that this involves an *intrinsic* relationship. The gift of God's grace neither interrupts nature nor simply adds to it. It permeates it in order to complete it. The entire natural order is thus to be understood as being "within" the supernatural. Moreover, this is in no way static. There is a profound dynamism here: the lure of divine grace imparts to the whole created order, set in time and history, an élan which generates the diversity and restlessness of human culture. In the case of human beings made in the image of God, our natural orientation to the supernatural indicates the presence of the divine in our depths. Humans always participate in God, and the continuing gift is a participatory putting on of Christ or the new nature, as is clear from the New Testament at Romans 13:14; Galatians 3:27; Ephesians 4:22–4; Colossians 3:12–17. 2 Peter 1:4 even tells us that through the very great promises of God "you may . . . become partakers of the divine nature".

De Lubac offers an integral vision with the widest possible horizon— his vision of a truly catholic Church. His opposition to narrowness and rigidity stems from this inclusive vision. Simply by virtue of God's creation he sees bonds of solidarity between all people, and he believes (this is surely warranted by St John's Prologue) that God has constantly been active through the Word, guiding them towards maturity. Catholicism is thus necessarily social and historical in its essence and practice. There is an unlimited drive towards mutual reconciliation and peace for the whole creation. Just as all things have their radical origin in God, so all creatures are being drawn back to God as their final destiny, where all is entirely natural and all entirely of grace, thus guaranteeing the integrity of each.

At the centre of this vision is the mystery of Christ, in whom all the promises of God are brought to fulfilment. Uniquely true God and true man, through his Incarnation, life, death and resurrection he brought into being the Church, which is oriented simultaneously to God and to the world: it is both called by God and a gathering of persons whose missionary task as Christ's body is to draw the whole world into a unity in Christ.

Thus the integralist points to this intrinsic relation of nature to supernature, as the most profound way of guaranteeing the integrity of each. The whole created order, set in time and history, is centred in Christ, and exhibits a cultural dynamism which moves towards a final unity-in-diversity. There is thus no god of arbitrary power bent on displacing or crushing our humanity.

This affects how the various disciplines are seen to relate to one another. Henri de Lubac's vision is clearly a rejection of sharp dualistic compartmentalizing into separate realms. The position he adopts has been called the "suspended middle". We live within the mystery of a free, gracious and dynamic God. De Lubac himself found that he could not practise philosophy without it transcending into theology, nor theology without it passing into philosophy. He constantly engaged with other disciplines too, including science (he was a great friend and supporter of Teilhard de Chardin). So the Christian must enter into open dialogue with a pluralist society, in a quest for truth which for ever remains incomplete. (In this sketch I have relied on Hans Urs von Balthasar, *The Theology of Henri de Lubac*; and John Milbank, *The Suspended Middle: Henri de Lubac and the Renewed Split in Modern Catholic Theology*, second edition.)

This integral vision is ultimately rooted in the Fathers of the early undivided Church, so its recovery is of huge significance for relations between the Western Church and Eastern Orthodoxy. The character and significance of this integralist approach will become clearer particularly in Part 4, when we explore the version of it contained in the vision of Rowan Williams, who draws particularly on the Greek Father St Maximus the Confessor.

Integralist practice

So how might an integralist approach (or a dialogic one like Temple's) be practised in the public arena today? I here draw on Elaine Graham's book *Between a Rock and a Hard Place: Public Theology in a Post-Secular Age*. I have refused to accept the widespread view that Christianity is addressed only to individuals, and that if it has anything to say to the public realm it can only do so through an individualistic morality. I also refuse to accept the division in liberal secular states between the public and private realms, such that Christians are required to bracket out their religious language from public discourse and adopt a shared universal and rational language. It has to be said that the secularist position is not neutral but has fundamental commitments antipathetic to religion. We then have to investigate what those commitments are and whether they will yield an adequate account of rationality for us and give us a "thick" enough body of knowledge to sustain our shared communal life. If a shrunken kind of thinking invades every aspect of human life, it is corrosive; for instance, putting a price on everything blots out any sense of society's public goods as transcending the status of commodities, and undermines the nature of democratic society itself.[24]

So Christians have to refuse to inhabit a private ghetto or set their deepest convictions aside when they enter the public arena. After all, there is no world in abstraction from God the Creator. They should be there in the public square, the marketplace of ideas, engaging in deed and word in matters of public concern, playing their part in forging a cohesive civil society. This implies respect for the insights of secular reason, in a way which is critical and constructive. This process has been called an "apologetics of presence", which will be not so much grounded in propositions as aiming at transformation: a kind of practical wisdom that seeks to show the difference that inhabiting Christian practice makes. It will therefore be most effective through the witness of local communities, and largely be the work of the laity. Statements by church leaders are not enough. We need the building up of the grass-roots practices of discipleship, covering worship, reflection and active citizenship.

All this assumes that Christian practice is never just a matter of individual and private devotion but carries over into the believer's life in all aspects of the public domain. It involves deep questions about the way things are and ought to be, necessary in the guidance of individual souls, societies and indeed the community of nations.[25] Needless to say, this is the sort of spirit which should animate any approach to people of another religion or none. To demand, for example (I take a case known to me), that a Japanese repudiate and root out Shinto and Buddhism from her life in order to embrace Christianity is profoundly insensitive and inhumane.

So we turn in Parts 3 and 4 to a fuller account of an integralist understanding of Christianity. Part 3 focusses on its principal act of worship; Part 4 sets out an understanding of the faith.

Notes

1. Jeremy Lent, *The Patterning Instinct: A Cultural History of Humanity's Search for Meaning*, p. 147.
2. Lent, *Patterning Instinct*, pp. 143, 150–4.
3. Lent, *Patterning Instinct*, pp. 154–6; the passage from the *Phaedo* is at 65c–66e.
4. Lent, *Patterning Instinct*, pp. 156f.
5. Plato, *The Republic*, 595–608.
6. Lent, *Patterning Instinct*, pp. 158f.
7. William R. Crockett, *Eucharist: Symbol of Transformation*, p. 82.
8. Lent, *Patterning Instinct*, p. 143.
9. Lent, *Patterning Instinct*, pp. 227f.
10. Lent, *Patterning Instinct*, pp. 229–31.
11. Pindar, *Nemean Odes*, VI. 1–7.
12. C. M. Bowra, *The Greek Experience*, pp. 44–6.
13. Patrick Whitworth, *Three Wise Men from the East: The Cappadocian Fathers and the Struggle for Orthodoxy*, p. 22, and see the whole of Chapter 2, "Through the Platonic Lens: The World of Hellenic Ideas".
14. Whitworth, *Three Wise Men from the East*, pp. 125–30.
15. William Temple, *Nature, Man and God*, pp. 366–8, 372–5, 395–7, his italics; cf. *Christianity and Social Order*, pp. 36f.
16. René Descartes, *Discourse on Method and The Meditations*, pp. 113, 53f.

17 Descartes, *Discourse on Method and The Meditations*, p. 54.
18 Lent, *Patterning Instinct*, pp. 235–8.
19 Arthur R. Peacocke, *Creation and the World of Science*, pp. 62f.
20 Madeleine Bunting, *Love of Country: A Hebridean Journey*, pp. 137, 148f.
21 David Olusoga, *Black and British: A Forgotten History*, pp. 121–42 (quotation at p. 124), 169–90.
22 Margaret Thatcher, Speech to the General Assembly of the Church of Scotland, 21 May 1988, on the website of the Thatcher Foundation.
23 William Temple, *Readings in St John's Gospel*, p. 48, his italics.
24 Elaine Graham, *Between a Rock and a Hard Place: Public Theology in a Post-Secular Age*, pp. 15f., 63, 89.
25 Graham, *Between a Rock and a Hard Place*, pp. xxii–xxvii, 16f., 185f., 210f. See too the forceful remarks of Rowan Williams on secularism, faith and freedom in *Faith in the Public Square*, p. 36.

PART 3

The Liturgy

I said in Part 2 that the roots of an integralist approach lie in the Church of the first five centuries. Within the biblical witness one of the finest instances, full of vivid images, is the first three chapters of the Pauline Letter to the Ephesians. The source of redemption is God the Father, who has made known his mysterious purpose for the fullness of time, to unite all things in heaven and earth. God's power has been shown decisively in Christ, in his life and death, resurrection and ascension to a position far above all other powers. God "has made him the head over all things for the church, which is his body, the fulness of him who fills all in all" (Ephesians 1:22–3). There is a dynamic process, in the here and now. For God in his great mercy and love has broken down the barriers of death, alienation and hostility to make people alive, at peace with God, reconciled to God and to each other in Christ, themselves raised up and exalted with Christ. So they are now members of the household of God, a building with Jesus Christ as the chief cornerstone, which "grows into a holy temple in the Lord; in whom you also are built into it for a dwelling place of God in the Spirit" (Ephesians 2:21–2). Further striking passages in Paul are Romans 8:18–39 and 1 Corinthians 15.

To take another instance, right at the start of St John's Gospel the one who was with God and was God in the beginning becomes incarnate, and a central theme is the offer of new life in place of death and the transition from death to life for those who trust in him. In Chapter 6, this is presented as effected only if one feeds on Christ. The ministry reaches its climax with the raising of Lazarus, which leads straight into the Passion, where the farewell discourse, such as on the vine and the branches, culminates in the great prayer of Christ to the Father in Chapter 17: "that they may be one, even as we are one" (17:11). The few with him stand for those who are yet to believe. For it is the world which is so loved by God (3:16), the world which is judged, and the world which is to be drawn to Christ lifted up on the cross (12:31f.; see also 10:10–16, 11:51f.).

In the Christian life the first response is worship: "Blessed be the God and Father of our Lord Jesus Christ, who has blessed us in Christ with every spiritual blessing in the heavenly places . . . " (Ephesians 1:3). In Christian worship, it is the Liturgy which comes to embody and enact this story in its fullest form. The word "liturgy" means "the work of the people". For centuries, it has consisted of two parts. First comes the Liturgy of the Word (the Greek word is *synaxis* = gathering, that is, of the *ekklesia* = the assembly duly summoned). This is followed by the Liturgy of the Sacrament / Liturgy of the Eucharist (*eucharistia* = thanksgiving), at the heart of which is the great thanksgiving prayer.

The Liturgy is in essence action, performance; it is not to be equated simply with its text. It is a cultural practice, a particular form of mobile knowing in time, which we encountered in Part 1. It resembles the acting of a drama or the playing of a musical score. It is rich in the use of symbols and requires continual re-enacting for its meaning to be realized. It is the action of a community of persons, like a theatre company or orchestra, each with their role to play as they enter into its movement and grow into its significance and truth.

The Liturgy is distinctive in that it is, at its very root, one with the movement of God within the Trinity and towards God's creation. It is the concentrated acting out of the Christian story of what God has done for creation, and particularly for the human race. It is eschatological, enacted in the time between the Incarnation, life, death and resurrection of Jesus Christ and the completion of God's Kingdom, where all things will be drawn into a final unity-in-diversity. Its members gather, bringing with them tokens of their ordinary life in the world, bread and wine, and opening themselves to the renewal of their lives, in order to become more fully what they already are by baptism, the body of Christ. At the same time, they are inviting the world to see its own true life and destiny in that movement and to allow itself to be drawn into the orbit of God's inexhaustible love. The appropriation of the meaning of the Liturgy is necessarily unending, since it is inseparable from the finite and fallible life of the world and from the unwavering action of God, who remains a mystery.

I shall now present two key biblical moments in the development of Christian worship, and then give a reconstruction of the likely shape and content of the Liturgy in the third century, before turning to the work of Gregory Dix on the shape of the Liturgy.

Division at Corinth

The oldest evidence of gathering to break bread is in St Paul's first letter to the Christians at Corinth, written somewhere in the 50s of the first century. He begins by assuring them that they are "called to be saints together with all those who in every place call on the name of our Lord Jesus Christ, both their Lord and ours" (1 Corinthians 1:2). But this is also already a critique; for they are riven by factions and at loggerheads among themselves. He appeals to them to be "united in the same mind and the same judgment" (1:10). It is God, not humans, who gave the growth and built the Church (3:6–9). And Christ is the power of God and the wisdom of God, and he cannot be divided (1:24,13).

Paul castigates them especially for when they "come together" as a church. "It is not the Lord's supper that you eat. For in eating, each one goes ahead with his own meal, and one is hungry and another is drunk. What! Do you not have houses to eat and drink in? Or do you despise the church of God and humiliate those who have nothing?" (11:20–22). As his own authority is impugned by the factions, he emphasizes the authenticity of the tradition into which he has initiated them:

> For I received from the Lord what I also delivered to you, that the Lord Jesus on the night when he was betrayed took bread, and when he had given thanks, he broke it, and said, "This is my body which is for you. Do this in remembrance of me." In the same way also the cup, after supper, saying, "This cup is the new covenant in my blood. Do this, as often as you drink it, in remembrance of me." For as often as you eat this bread and drink the cup, you proclaim the Lord's death until he comes (11:23–26).

Members must therefore first examine themselves. "For any one who eats and drinks without discerning the body eats and drinks judgment upon himself" (11:29). They are "guilty of profaning the body and blood of the Lord" (11:27).

Several points here deserve attention. First, this failure to discern is not just mental or spiritual. It has shown itself in members being weak and ill, and even dying (11:30). This is a typically Jewish outlook: soul and body are dimensions of a single person. In modern parlance, we are a psycho-somatic unity. This stands in contrast to the prevalence in surrounding cultures of some form of dualism which separates out these dimensions or sets them in opposition.

Paul has already closely related this thought to the Liturgy. "The cup of blessing which we bless, is it not a participation [or communion] in the blood of Christ? The bread which we break, is it not a participation in the body of Christ? Because there is one loaf, we who are many are one body, for we all partake of the one loaf." Therefore, says Paul, Christians must shun idol worship. True, idols are nothing. But it is a sheer contradiction to worship God and worship idols (10:14–21). Both are participatory practices, not just purely mental or spiritual transactions.

This tallies with the letter sent by the apostles and elders to the churches after conferring in Jerusalem (Acts 15:29). As we shall see, this outlook was crucial in maintaining the integrity of the life of the Church in the public realm. Moreover, that letter also instructs them to avoid unchastity, which is matched in 1 Corinthians by Paul's injunction, "Glorify God in your body" (1 Corinthians 6:12–20). Integrity was to be maintained too in intimate personal relations. Thus the Lordship of Christ covered the whole of life.

It is worth noting here that 1 Corinthians points to a very close nexus of three senses of the term "body". There is the body of Christ offered on Calvary; the body and blood in the Liturgy; and the Church, which is the body of Christ. When Paul speaks of profaning the body and blood by failing to discern the body, it is usually taken to refer to the second of these. But it could equally refer back to the despising of the Church and the humiliation of those who have nothing (cf. Matthew 25:31–46). And the very next chapter is given over to expounding the varieties of gifts, but the same Spirit; varieties of service, but the same Lord; and varieties of working, but the same God who inspires them all in everyone. "For just as the body is one and has many members, and all the members of the body, though many, are one body, so it is with Christ. For by one Spirit we were all baptized into one body—Jews or Greeks, slaves or free—and all were made to drink of one Spirit" (1 Corinthians 12:4–31; see also Romans 12:4–7).

The urgency of the situation is clear to Paul. It is eschatological: we are living in the last days, between the decisive coming of Jesus Christ in history and his final coming. There will be a judgment at the end, but this is plainly already at work in the present, not only confronting the Jews and the rest of humanity, but also pressing constantly upon Christians themselves.

Pentecost and its significance

St Luke, the companion of Paul and author of the Gospel in his name as well as the Acts of the Apostles, clearly selected and ordered his material around his concerns. He was an apologist for Christianity. The first work reaches its climax with the rooting of the Church in Jerusalem, the second with its establishment in Rome. He probably wrote around the years 80–90. Whilst relying no doubt on eyewitnesses, his account of Pentecost is part of a well-developed salvation history.

St Luke tells us that on the day of Pentecost the twelve apostles "were all together in one place". A sound like the rush of a roaring gale came upon them and filled all the house, and separate tongues of fire rested on each of them. "And they were all filled with the Holy Spirit" (Acts 2:1–4). "At this sound the multitude came together, and they were bewildered, because each one heard them speaking in his own language" (Acts 2:6). St Peter's speech (Acts 2:14–36) is a presentation of the significance of Pentecost. It was the final vindication of Jesus as God's Messiah: God had raised him up and exalted him, and now Jesus' confirmation of the promise of the Holy Spirit (see Acts 1:4–5) had been fulfilled. "Let all the house of Israel therefore know assuredly that God has made him both Lord and Christ, this Jesus whom you crucified."

Pentecost is the fulfilment of Old Testament prophecy, specifically that of Joel. God had promised through him, "I will pour out my Spirit on all flesh; your sons and your daughters shall prophesy, your old men shall dream dreams, and your young men shall see visions" (Joel 2:28). Moreover, this man Jesus is of universal significance, both in time and space. Joel's prophecy is eschatological: it is about "the last days ... before the day of the Lord" (Acts 2:17–20), which is the decisive and final reckoning or judgment. In terms of space, Joel foresees the Spirit poured out "upon all flesh" (Acts 2:17). This is already clear when the apostles speak in other languages, since it heralds the reversal of God's scattering of people over the face of all the earth at the end of the story of the Tower of Babel (Genesis 11:1–9). Peter appeals to his hearers to repent, be baptized in the name of Jesus Christ for the forgiveness of sins and receive the gift of the Holy Spirit. For the promise is not only to all the Jewish diaspora, but also "to all that are far off, every one whom the Lord our God calls" (Acts 2:39). Pentecost is the assurance that all will be brought by God into full unity.

From that day

> they devoted themselves to the apostles' teaching and fellowship, to the breaking of bread and the prayers ... And all who believed were together and had all things in common; and they sold their possessions and goods and distributed them to all, as any had need. And day by day, attending the temple together and breaking bread in their homes, they partook of food with glad and generous hearts, praising God and having favour with all the people (Acts 2:42–7).

As faithful Jews they attended the temple in Jerusalem, but the centre was their homes. The double reference to the breaking of bread points towards ordinary meals being invested with new meaning connected with Jesus' fellowship meals, culminating in the Last Supper.

Westerners with the New Testament before them naturally think of the journeys of St Paul in the Graeco-Roman world. But the early Christians also quickly spread south towards Africa and right across the Middle East. Here they set about one of the most ambitious and far-reaching missionary programmes in history. There was an archbishop in Kashgar, the oasis town where the main trade route east passed into China, long before there was an archbishop in Canterbury. Even in the Middle Ages there were more Christians in Asia than in Europe.[1]

As the Church spread outwards in all directions, it increasingly provoked the hostility of the Jews, so the connection with the temple became more fraught and tenuous and was severed in any case in the year 70: after a major Jewish revolt had failed, the Romans demolished it. Yet all Christian worship remained rooted and saturated in Jewish worship.

Let us now imagine a city somewhere in the vast Roman Empire. There is a small Christian community there. It is near the end of the third century. What might well have been the pattern and content of their worship? Let us imagine a seeker, Julia. (I draw here particularly on A. E. Welsford, *Life in the Early Church A.D. 33–313*, especially pp. 225–42.)

Julia at the *synaxis*

Julia is already impressed with the little she knows about the Christian story and what she has seen of Christian conduct. She approaches two Christian friends for further exploration and guidance. They realize she is in earnest and arrange to take her to the Christian service. They call for her before dawn on Sunday morning and take her through the streets to a large house built in the traditional Roman style, the home of the widow of a wine merchant. Julia notices that there is a deacon at the door, checking their identity. The friends vouch for her. They enter a large rectangular room (*atrium*), with aisles down each side. Here there are dozens of men and women chatting in little groups, waiting for the service to begin. Julia's friends take her forward to the far end of the room and up two steps to a dais (*tablinum*), to present her to a man sitting in an armchair in ordinary clothes and a group of men sitting in an arc on either side of him. This is the bishop and the presbyters. As Julia returns towards the entrance, she notices just below the dais a stone table (*cartibulum*) which will be used as the table for communion. The middle of the room is open to the sky, with a rain-water tank (*impluvium*), which is used at times for baptisms. As she is a seeker, she must take her place at the back of the room with other enquirers and those preparing for membership (catechumens). Her friends now leave her there and join the full members, with men on one side and women on the other.

Two deacons standing on either side of the bishop now signal to the congregation to be silent, as the service is about to begin. The first part is modelled on the worship of the Jewish synagogue, and it is known as the *synaxis* (from the same Greek root). The bishop greets the people, and they reply. A reader now stands at a lectern and intones a reading from the Old Testament. Then a soloist sings a psalm, and the congregation respond in unison. There is a passage from a letter by St Paul, and another psalm. Then there is the intoning of the Gospel. The bishop, remaining seated, expounds the meaning of the scriptures which have been read.

Then one of the deacons calls out, "Bow down your heads for a blessing, O catechumens." The bishop gives the catechumens and seekers a blessing, and the deacon cries out, "Let the catechumens depart. Let no catechumen remain." For the intercessions, which are made in the power of the Spirit and in union with Christ, and then the Eucharist are now to follow.

Julia as a catechumen

So Julia leaves, pondering all she has heard and seen. She decides to ask to be admitted to the catechumenate, supported by her friends as sponsors, and goes through a long process of instruction in the faith. This includes exorcism. We saw how St Paul discussed worship of God and worship of idols. On the one hand the power of idols was nothing. Yet traditional religion still had a huge hold on the vast majority of the population of the Graeco-Roman world, and all manner of cults had long been pouring into it, especially from the east. These varieties of religion were deeply engrained in the culture, embracing both belief and conduct. So exorcism was not, as we might suppose, about casting out a ghost from some troubled individual. It was to do with the fundamental need to be loyal to Christ and being able to discern when and how to obey God rather than humans (cf. Acts 4:12, 19f.; John 12:42f.).

Julia learns that admission to full membership of the Church takes place at its annual celebration of Pascha. As Pascha approaches, she goes through an intensive preparation in what was becoming the season of Lent. At the right time, she goes through the ceremony of the "Opening of the Ears", in Latin *"Traditio Symboli"*—the "Handing over of the Symbol" or password. This was almost certainly in essence the Apostles' Creed. It was a simple statement of belief in God the Father, Son and Holy Spirit, and of the main facts about the Lord Jesus Christ. The idea is taken from army life and discipline and emphasized the need for loyalty and devotion to the service of Christ. At this ceremony, which usually took place on Maundy Thursday, the catechumen stood up before the congregation, renounced the devil, and declared the faith by repeating the Creed.

Pascha

This whole period was a time of fasting and prayer by the catechumens, their sponsors, and the whole congregation. Pascha was celebrated as the great festival of redemption, the great passing over. The whole church gathered on the Saturday evening to keep vigil together until the dawn of Easter morning. The night was filled with many readings from the Old Testament, focussed on God's mighty acts of deliverance: the creation, the deliverance of Noah, Abraham's sacrifice of Isaac, the passage of the Israelites through the Red Sea, Ezekiel's vision of the valley of the dry bones coming to life, Jonah's three days in the belly of the whale. The final Old Testament reading was the story of the Passover itself, and the command for it to be celebrated for all generations by the nation (Exodus 12). The last lesson was always the Passion according to St John, right up to the resurrection. The bishop began his sermon, and Julia listened to an exposition of St Paul's words: "Christ, our paschal lamb, has been sacrificed" (1 Corinthians 5:7).

The candidates with their sponsors then withdrew to a room where they were stripped of their outer garments. They affirmed their belief in God, Father, Son and Holy Spirit, and stepped into a shallow basin or pool which served as a font. The bishop poured water over their heads three times, saying, "I baptize you in the name of the Father, and of the Son, and of the Holy Spirit." After that the sponsors led them away and clothed them in the white garments of newborn members (neophytes).

Confirmation immediately followed: the bishop laid his hands on each neophyte, saying, "In the name of the Father, and of the Son, and of the Holy Spirit. Peace be with you." They were anointed with consecrated oil (chrism) and given the kiss of peace. They were now members and could join fully in Christian worship. And so Julia moved into her first communion, just as dawn broke.

The doors are now already shut, with only the full members present. They all stand for the intercessions, and the bishop leads them. He first prays for the holy Church of God to be kept in peace, unity and safety throughout the world, with the principalities and powers subjected to it, so that it spends all its days in peace and quietness to the glory of God. Then one of the deacons calls on all to bow the knee in silent prayer. The bishop sums up the prayer in a collect. Similarly prayers are offered for the civil government, for the sick, and for the newly baptized.

It is then that the Liturgy of the Eucharist begins. The bishop greets the people with the words, "Peace be with you", and all exchange the kiss of peace with their neighbours. The two deacons bring a white linen cloth to cover the stone table at the foot of the dais. Others collect the offerings which the people have brought: little loaves of bread and some wine in a flask. The deacons place the offerings on the table, and the bishop steps down from the dais and stands facing the people across the table, with the presbyters grouped around him. They add their gifts, and the bishop blesses the offerings.

He then says, "Lift up your hearts", and the people reply, "We lift them up to the Lord." He says, "Let us give thanks to the Lord", and they reply, "It is meet and right." The bishop then intones the great prayer of thanksgiving, addressing God the Father. He rehearses in his own words the traditional themes, from the creation of the world to the Incarnation, the cross, the resurrection and the ascension. He recalls the Last Supper and the words of Christ instituting the Eucharist. He offers the bread and wine in remembrance (*anamnesis*) of Christ: not only his death but also his resurrection and ascension, until he comes. He prays that all who partake might be made one and be filled with the Holy Spirit and ends by praying that through Christ and in the Holy Spirit all honour and glory be given to God, for ever and world without end.

The congregation assent with a loud "Amen". Then the bishop breaks some of the bread and makes his communion, followed by the presbyters and deacons. The deacons further break up the bread for the communion of the laity. There are also three chalices, one of wine mixed with a little water, one of water, and one of milk and honey, symbolizing entry into the Promised Land of God's kingdom. Then the laity come up in single file and stand to receive the bread, and then pass on to where deacons stand holding the chalices. They sip from each.

The deacons then receive fragments of the bread to take to the sick. Some of the laity also come up to receive fragments, which they take home to consume during the week, as part of their personal devotions.

Finally, once the vessels have been cleaned, one of the deacons declares, "Go in peace", and the congregation quietly depart to their homes.

Julia will wear her white robes right through to the other major festival for Christians, Pentecost. Just as the Jews treated Passover to Pentecost as a continuous period of rejoicing in the deliverance from Egypt and the occupation of the Promised Land, so Christians celebrated continuously from Pascha to Pentecost their redemption and entry into the Kingdom of God.

Julia's Christian life

Julia also learned about the growing practice of private prayer. The whole day was coming to be punctuated by regular prayer; Wednesdays and Fridays became fast days; and grace was regularly said at meals. All these practices were taken over and adapted from Judaism (cf. Cornelius in Acts 10:1–3, 30). They were not obligatory, but they did express the conviction that their faith covered the whole of life.

And maybe Julia had occasions to travel. Wherever she went, she would have been welcomed by the Christian congregation as a sister in Christ and invited to join them in the celebration of the Eucharist. There were different languages spoken, but she would still have been able to follow the action of the rite. As we shall see, the worship was not uniform, and different areas developed their own practices and ethos. But they also constantly strove to keep in touch with each other, because they knew they were one in Christ and charged to draw the whole world into a unity. In the very early *Didache* (*Teaching of the Twelve Apostles*), there is a beautiful prayer which includes the words, "As this broken [bread] was scattered upon the tops of the mountains and being gathered became one, so gather Thy church from the ends of the earth into Thy kingdom; for Thine is the glory and the power through Jesus Christ for ever."[2] Julia would recognize in the action a consistent shape. The diversity was quite capable of being consonant with the conviction that they were all members of one body. If Christians today have a similar experience, it is because they benefit from more than a century of study of the Liturgy, so that ecumenically the pattern and content are very similar.

Gregory Dix on the shape of the Liturgy

Gregory Dix focussed primarily on the Liturgy of the Eucharist. His fundamental claim was that the early Christians grasped that it is not primarily something *said*, but something *done*: they habitually spoke of "doing the Eucharist", "performing the mysteries", "doing the oblation". It is a coming together, a corporate rite; it is a single action in which different participants perform complementary roles, as the work of the People of God.[3]

This single action is at its heart four-fold: the offertory; the thanksgiving; the breaking of the bread (the fraction); and the communion. The offertory is the special liturgy of the laity: they provide the bread and wine. Then comes the great prayer of thanksgiving, which is the special liturgy of the celebrant, normally in those days the bishop; then comes the breaking of the bread, principally by the celebrant; and then all receive both the bread and the wine. Throughout the service the deacons perform various assisting tasks.

Dix discusses at length the relation of the Last Supper to the shape and content of the Eucharist. He observes that at the Last Supper there is a seven-fold action: Jesus takes bread, gives thanks over it, breaks it and distributes it; later in the meal he takes the cup, gives thanks over it, and gives it to all to drink. Dix finds absolutely no case where this pattern is preserved in the shape of the Liturgy; the Church universally saw fit to concentrate it into a four-fold action.[4]

Clearly the Last Supper was on Thursday (by our reckoning), Jesus was crucified on Friday, and his body was hurriedly placed in a tomb before the Sabbath (Saturday) began. It seems from John (19:14, 31, 42) that the Friday was a day of Preparation not only for the Sabbath but also in that year for the Passover. Mark, Matthew and Luke take the Last Supper to be a Passover meal, whereas John places it before the Passover (13:1). Dix thought John to be correct and noted that his Eucharistic teaching is mainly found in Chapter 6, where Jesus feeds the multitude with loaves and fishes and declares that he is the Bread of Life (6:35, 41). Whatever the truth here, there was a confluence of two streams, both of them very Jewish. There are the Passover themes of God's liberation of slaves and the formation of a people under the Law, together with the sacrifice of a lamb to be corporately eaten. And there are the regular meals of Jesus with his followers—actually with all and sundry—of which this is the last.

Dix held that Jesus did not institute an entirely new rite. His actions are rooted in Jewish tradition, but by what he had said over the bread and the cup he had given a profoundly new meaning to his actions. The command was, "Do this in remembrance of me." What is to be remembered is no doubt focally his death, but "of me" surely points to his whole person and action. The early Christians right from the start understood that Jesus was not just instructing them to give thanks over bread and wine—they would do that anyway—but to be obedient to what he had commanded them to do. So the Eucharist was from the first intensely concentrated on fulfilling that command. It had a directness which was focussed on what God had done in Christ, without devotional elaborations of any kind whatever.[5]

It is vital at this point to grasp the meaning of the word "*anamnesis*", the Greek word we translate as "remembrance". Today, when we remember or recall, we usually see it as a mental transaction, a bringing back to mind of something we have forgotten or have not been thinking about. In the ancient world both Hebrew and Greek thought was rather different. In Hebrew traditions, when people remember, they are entering into what

God has done for them (Deuteronomy 5:15, 32:7; 1 Chronicles 16:12). Often they appeal to God to remember the covenant between God and Israel. When the Israelites are oppressed as slaves in Egypt, their cry comes up to God. God remembers his covenant with Abraham, Isaac and Jacob by activating it in the deliverance from bondage (Exodus 2:23–5). In the Greek-speaking world, *anamnesis* was also understood in a dynamic sense: not as mentally retrieving something absent, but as an active re-calling or re-presenting of something so that it is *presently operative* by its effects. In Christian terms, God takes a fresh and decisive initiative in Christ, who recreates the covenant community by his death once for all and by his resurrection and ascension to heaven, where he continually presents his sacrifice to the Father. In the Liturgy, Christians re-present before God the one sacrifice of Christ in all its completeness, so that it is here and now effectual in them. That is, the Church which is his body repeatedly re-calls Christ's life before God and enters into the movement of his self-offering in order to be nourished and energized more and more as that body. The members are continually to become what they already are by baptism.

It is thus a relational process, and it is highly complex. We saw earlier how Paul understood "the body of Christ" in three closely related senses: the body of Christ himself during his life and death on Calvary; the body and blood associated with the elements of bread and wine in the Liturgy; and the Church as the body of Christ. For the Greek Fathers and for Augustine, there is an indissoluble unity of the Eucharist with the once-for-all sacrifice of Christ himself. Dix quotes two notable passages in Augustine: "So the Lord willed to impart his body, and his blood which he shed for the remission of sins. If you have received well, you *are* that which you have received" (*Sermon* 227). "Your mystery is laid on the table of the Lord, your mystery you receive. To that which you are you answer 'Amen', and in answering you assent. For you hear the words, 'The body of Christ' and you answer 'Amen'. Be a member of the body of Christ, that the 'Amen' be true" (*Sermon* 272). For there is one Lord Jesus Christ, across all those senses of body. He is present as the Offerer, who offers himself through the Church his body. This connects with what I said earlier in Part 2, that symbols in the ancient world participate in what they symbolize. There is a unity between symbol and reality.

Participation in the Eucharist meant participation in the body and blood of Christ himself, both through the symbols of bread and wine and in his body the Church.[6] This also fits well with an integralist view of how humans participate in God, as God's grace permeates the natural order.

Criticisms of Gregory Dix

Study in the last seventy-five years shows that the historical context of the early centuries of the Church contributing to the shape of the Eucharist was more complex than Dix recognized, and that his fundamental claims were expressed too schematically. Paul F. Bradshaw and Maxwell E. Johnson point out that the whole Graeco-Roman world had for centuries held feasts and drinking parties with a measure of formality, which invariably included rituals honouring the gods. And though the Jews were distinctive in their fidelity, they did mingle with other cultures, particularly so in the diaspora. The earliest meals shared among Christians appear to have taken varying forms rather than following a single standard pattern. This would reflect cultural diversity, as well as whether the meal was hosted within a wealthier person's house or was a gathering of the impoverished.[7]

Dix tied the origin of the Eucharist very closely to the Last Supper: the focus is on the association of the bread and wine with the body and blood of Christ and the command "Do this", leading directly to the standard four-fold structure. For him, the full meal seen at Corinth was already a rite, different from ordinary meals at home, and well before the end of the first century it had been separated into an *Agape* (Love Feast) and the clear-cut concentrated rite and order of the Eucharist. But this separation was a much slower process. Indeed it looks as if there was a whole range of corporate meals eaten, from the ordinary to the much more formal, which were reoriented so that the participants now remembered the Christian story.

It is also worth noting that the Passover meal in Matthew, Mark and Luke is originally focussed more on the betrayal and on Jesus' saying that he will not drink the fruit of the vine until he drinks it new in the Kingdom of God. The words over the bread and cup seem to have been grafted on later. Indeed, the words, "Do this in remembrance of me" do not appear in their accounts (except at Luke 22:19, but the RSV doubts it is original). They are found only in Paul's account in 1 Corinthians 11, which is the first witness to the idea that the Christian meal is a commemoration of Christ's passion (cf. 1 Corinthians 5:7: "Christ, our paschal lamb, has been sacrificed").

The close connection Dix sees with Christ's sacrificial death is not always present in early Christian practice. The idea of sacrifice was certainly there in a broader sense. Christians were conscious that the sacrificial system in the temple was superseded. They often spoke of theirs being a "sacrifice of praise and thanksgiving", and "a bloodless sacrifice and spiritual worship", and focussed on the need to be morally pure in order to come before God (cf. Matthew 5:23f.). Irenaeus does speak of the bread and cup being offered to God, but he is thinking more of a thank-offering of the first fruits (Deuteronomy 26:1–11). It appears that it was out of such interpretations that the bread and cup were thought of as "oblations". This was no doubt encouraged by the fact that the participants in the Eucharist continued to bring these gifts with them.[8]

So the context of the development of the Liturgy was rather more complex than Dix recognized, and its shape and meaning more diverse and fluid. Nevertheless, Dix's work marks the recovery of the liturgical understanding which became prevalent within the Church of the first five centuries. It clearly has affinities with an integralist approach and is of great importance in any quest for an adequate view of the Liturgy today and its relation to the world.

"Are you a Christian?"

But perhaps Julia did not travel; perhaps her life was cut short. For most of the first three centuries, from Nero's decree in 64 to Diocletian, who reigned from 284–305, simply to be a Christian was a capital offence, with summary execution, unless it was commuted to penal servitude for life, maybe in the lead mines of Sardinia. Roman emperors constantly feared insubordination and strove to hold their sprawling territories together.

They behaved like any totalitarian government: they did not care what people believed privately and individually; the crux was whether they acted publicly on that belief. It was precisely here that they suspected and feared the Church. For it insisted on the necessity of regular corporate worship. It settled on a long preparation by catechumens before baptism and confirmation, which alone admitted a person to pray with the Church, let alone do the Eucharist. The penalty for apostasy was lifelong exclusion from the corporate life of the Church. They met in private houses behind closed doors. It therefore had all the appearance of a secretive association. The Christians could not easily respond by holding the rite in public. It was not just that the practice of the faith was a capital offence. They also knew they were guardians of a revealed mystery (Ephesians 1:9f.). Jesus Christ was for them the only Saviour of humanity, drawing all people to himself by his sacrificial death; the Church was his body, the communion of redeemed sinners, corporately invested with Christ's mission of salvation to the whole world. The Christians were bound to see themselves as primarily over against the world, where the central issue was: whose lordship is to be obeyed?

The state devised a simple test of loyalty: burn incense before an image of the emperor. In fact the authorities often took a lenient view of the Christians, and magistrates would even plead with prisoners to fulfil the test. Full state-sponsored persecution was comparatively rare. The longest and worst was initiated by Diocletian, lasting ten years from 303. He had spent most of his reign saving the empire from chaos and refounding it on a basis of the old Roman virtues. Setting aside his reluctance, he vigorously persecuted the Church, because he saw in it a profound threat to all he had achieved.

However, the greater threat to Christians came from the populace, who did not so much fear them as hate them. For Christians, normal daily life could at any time suddenly be disrupted by a mob baying for blood. Its imagination ran riot over their likely activities: ritual murder, cannibalism, promiscuity and incest; its hatred was irrational. Justin and Tertullian tried defending the faith, the one by reasoned description, the other by passionate invective, but to no avail. Justin was himself martyred. Huge numbers suffered opposition from their families and ostracism from their neighbours. Yet more endured disabilities in their fortunes and their persons. And the malign mob or private informers denounced thousands of Christians to the magistrates. In Abilinitina in North Africa, the Christians as a body were distraught that the Eucharist had been lacking for a long time through the apostasy of their bishop. At the height of the Diocletian persecution, they were well aware of the primary need to celebrate but knew that the authorities were on the watch for them. In the end, they called on a presbyter to celebrate and took the risk of almost certain detection to assemble. They all paid the penalty for their faith.[9]

The great reversal

Diocletian abdicated in 305, but the persecution persisted, and brought the Church to the brink of extinction. But then came an amazing reversal.

In 306, Constantine was declared emperor in York. He contested the western half of the empire, and in 312 defeated his rival in battle in Italy. Already deeply impressed by the heroism of the Church under persecution, he claimed that before the battle he had been given a sign of favour by the Christian God: a vision of the cross with the assurance, "In this sign you shall conquer". Suddenly the Church was being freed of its disabilities, and he went on to legislate in its interests. In 323, he defeated Licinius, who ruled the eastern half, and so was left master of the whole empire. He built Constantinople as his new capital. Earlier emperors had sought to defend the empire against the threat of the Church. Now Constantine became its patron. He had churches erected, and pressed hard for unity within the Church, believing that a united empire needed a united Church to support it. In 325, he summoned the Council of Nicaea, which rejected Arianism by acknowledging the full divinity of Christ. He was eventually baptized on his deathbed in 337. So the Church, from being an illegal organization which was bound to remain essentially world-renouncing, was now welcomed and would experience a huge influx of enquirers and see the rise of a nominally Christian world.[10]

How was the Church to respond to this totally unprecedented situation? It could have striven to become an elite, whether in knowledge, spirituality or morality. But the early Church had always held that the gospel was absolutely for all. Its actual membership was from many different social groups, especially the poor and less educated, freedmen and slaves. The alternative path was to be open to the world. There the Church recognized the great danger of compromise with alien beliefs and morals, and of the lowering of Christian standards in faith and conduct.[11] But here was a great missionary opportunity, and it was hardly possible to reject it. So in the fourth century, we see a complex and multiple revolution, at the heart of which was worship.

Church and Liturgy in the fourth-century world

The Church needed to provide a public worship responsive to the new needs. Hitherto its worship had been that of a semi-secret sect; now it was becoming a public activity of the population at large. The issue was fundamentally whether a new relationship could be forged with integrity between Christian faith and the longstanding assumptions of the ancient world. It was a daunting task, for Christians were still in a minority and still living in a largely alien society. It is also worth remembering that Arius had tried to fuse Christian and Greek assumptions, and in spite of the decision at Nicaea the controversy was to rage on for most of the fourth century. At least the Church was now free to work openly within those conditions and did so in new and creative ways.[12]

As the Church came to feel more at home in the world, so it became more reconciled to time. In earlier centuries, Christians had known the world as primarily hostile and alien, and with good reason. They never knew whether they would be arrested and asked in court the fateful question, "Are you a Christian?" They had taken with full seriousness the eschatological belief that in Christ the day of the Lord had come, the new covenant had been given, and they were now living in the last days. The Liturgy showed them their true being as already in the midst of this life eternally redeemed and translated into the Kingdom of God and the World to come. Now Christians relaxed into a more positive view of the world.[13]

The Liturgy of the early Church had been a corporate act, intense, direct and concentrated on the action of God in Christ. This left little room for devotional practice: there were no devotions in preparation for communion, no confession of sin. Nor was there much place for this in the *synaxis*. Such devotions took place in the privacy of members' homes. Here they would give time for daily prayer and communicate from the bread they had brought home from the weekly Liturgy. As we saw, by the third century, a regular pattern of prayer was developing right across the day.[14]

In the fourth century, there was a great increase in this domestic prayer. This was partly an effect of the rise of monasticism. The early Christians had basically been world-renouncing. They were at odds with the claims of Caesar and the world around them, and had witnessed to the sole Lordship of Christ, often to the point of giving their lives as martyrs. Now, in response to the opening up of the Church to the world, huge numbers of Christians left their ordinary lives and made worship of God the end and aim of all their activities. Whether they lived as hermits or in monastic communities, they sought God for God's own sake—a novel lifestyle. It is important to be clear how they related to the early Christian outlook and to the contemporary Church. Though there were exceptions, for the most part they saw themselves as faithful members of the Church, loyal to its structure and its Liturgy. True, like the early Christians, they separated themselves from the life of the world. But they did not reject it as wholly in the power of evil. Rather it was still God's world, called to redemption. So they set themselves to bear witness to God's decisive action in Christ's life, death, resurrection and ascension, precisely in order to bring that world to God and sanctify it. In this way, they protected the Church from the dangers of worldliness which could engulf it. And one effect was that they inspired many of the laity to give themselves with great enthusiasm to a devout life of prayer whilst continuing to live in the world.[15]

As the monks had wholly given their lives to God, they had all day to focus on God, and this they filled with offices. These were essentially a development of the private devotion of the early Church. They consisted in a daily cycle of praise, reciting the psalms and canticles, and listening to readings, all designed to be edifying.[16]

These developments fed into public worship. At the same time, worship became more formal in style and incorporated rituals and symbols from the civic world to suit the new setting. Each of the traditional patriarchates of Rome, Antioch, Alexandria and Constantinople became influential centres, consolidating local practices and creating identities through distinct forms of liturgy, canon law and spirituality in their particular cultural contexts.[17] Jerusalem, under St Cyril, who became its bishop in about 350, unsurprisingly became a destination for pilgrimage, made fashionable by the visits of Constantine's mother, St Helena, and Constantine himself founded splendid churches at Calvary and the Mount of Olives. A whole round of daily offices from the Night Office to Vespers was instituted. So for the first time, the Church adopted into its corporate worship the monastic ideal of sanctifying human life as a whole. It is a process which Dix calls the sanctification of time. It marks the end of the earlier tradition, that corporate worship expressed primarily the enforced separation of the Church from the world.[18]

The fourth-century churches embarked on wholesale liturgical revision. Freed from persecution, the different churches were able to communicate with each other. They each took stock of their local traditions, sifted their devotional value and borrowed freely from each other. Ceremony became elaborated, for example at the entrance, at the presentation of the Eucharistic gifts, and over communion. Intercessions expanded; homilies became common.[19] In particular the great thanksgiving prayer had never had a fixed wording. It had been the office of the bishop in his own words to give praise for all God had done in Christ. Now on the one hand, it came to incorporate new expressions and expand, whilst on the other it gradually crystallized into a number of more fixed versions. The whole process raised the level of theological understanding of the faith and enabled the Church to express its Eucharistic devotion with a new precision and elegance of literary form.[20]

We also see the growth of a liturgical calendar and lectionaries. The observance of Sunday was not based on the Sabbath commandment in the Old Testament. Christians treated the ceremonial law as abrogated, including this one. The rabbis had made the Sabbath essentially a day of rest, in which abstinence from work was governed by minute regulation;

attendance at public worship was not essential. The Christians by contrast treated Sunday as an ordinary working day and attendance at worship as a requirement. Sunday is a festival. The Epistle of Barnabas (c.100–130) has God declaring that "I will make the beginning with the eighth day, which is the beginning of another world". Sunday is therefore clearly eschatological, representing the inauguration of the world to come. It is only secondarily a memorial of the resurrection of Jesus as a historical event. It is observed because in his resurrection and ascension Christians have really been transferred into the heavens in Christ, and he manifests himself to his own when the Church gathers. It was only the secular edict of Constantine in 321 making Sunday a public holiday which first based Christian observance of Sunday on the fourth commandment.[21]

The two main annual festivals in the early Church were Pascha and Pentecost. Both are clearly related to the Jewish feasts of the Passover (Hebrew: *Pesach*) and Pentecost. But whereas the Jewish feasts could occur on any day of the week, from quite early on they were observed by Christians on a Sunday.

The primitive Pascha was an eschatological liturgy of redemption. The redemption was not from bondage in Egypt, but from sin, time and mortality into "the glorious liberty of the children of God" (Romans 8:21) and "the eternal kingdom of our Lord and Saviour Jesus Christ" (2 Peter 1:11). His life, death, resurrection and ascension—the paschal sacrifice—was the means by which this redemption was achieved. It was a single event. And the identification of Christ with his Church in a single body was taken for granted. As Pascha dramatized the fact of eternal redemption, so Pentecost dramatized the Christian's possession of (or by) the Holy Spirit, which made that redemption an effective reality in this life in time. This is rather different from our Western practice of focussing in turn on the successive days of Maundy Thursday, Good Friday and the Day of Resurrection.[22]

Another important development was in the commemoration of saints' days, especially those who had been martyred. The earliest known is that of Polycarp, Bishop of Smyrna, martyred in 156. Commemorations were joyful occasions, celebrating the martyr's birthday into heaven. The relics of the martyrs were treasured, and their prayers, along with the angels', were sought for those still on earth. The idea of saints interceding before the throne of heaven was already present to the Jews in the second century BC, and nothing in the New Testament rejected it. Indeed, the eschatological notion that *all* Christians even in this world had been transferred to the heavenly realms in Christ would tend to make such a communion of saints more natural, reducing the sense of the barrier interposed by death. Now there was an increasing cult of local martyrs who had witnessed outstandingly for the Lordship of Christ against the world, and this enabled the Church to set forth Jesus as Lord not only of universal history but also of homely local history, which was a much more concrete notion for the ordinary person.[23]

Two other developments are of great importance. We saw how earlier a gathering of the Church would be in a large private house. In the fourth century, as the Church expanded, there was a huge growth in church buildings. These roughly retained the shape of the Roman house, but were modelled more on civic buildings, called basilicas. Many were built through the patronage of the emperor or high officials. They were often well furnished. This was certainly true of churches in Rome and Constantinople, but also of smaller cities. Even the house-churches of the earlier Church often had silver plate and other adornments. And we know that the one at Dura-Europos in Syria had a baptistry painted from floor to ceiling with pictures of scenes from the Old and New Testaments. Music and painting, incised chalices of precious metal and even sculpture were used in Christian worship by 250. As soon as the persecution was over, the Christians of Tyre built a church with cedar ceilings, delicately carved altar rails and mosaic pavements. So just because the Liturgy had a simple structure, it did not follow that the Christians practised a puritan bareness for its own sake. Indeed the Johannine book Revelation pictures heavenly worship as a reality faintly reproduced in the earthly worship of the Church. When Constantine gave full liberty for public worship, the Church thought it right to realize those heavenly ideals so far as possible on earth. Dix sees it as part of the general translation of worship from the idiom of eschatology into that of time.[24] It is surely more accurate to say that it was still eschatological but took a more positive view of life in time.

Going back further still, the Jerusalem temple was a beautiful building with elaborate ceremonial worship. Jesus had never condemned it on those grounds, and the early Christians continued to frequent it until they were driven out. Besides, the whole Graeco-Roman world firmly believed that magnificence was a virtue in public life. And countless people had proudly performed their civic *leitourgia* in contributing to the adornment of their cities.[25]

In the early Church, there was a single *ecclesia* in each city or area, that is, a single Eucharistic assembly of the whole local church under its own bishop and presbyters. As the Church rapidly expanded, this inevitably broke down. Presbyters, who had always been the bishop's deputies, were now ordained by the bishop to act for him in particular churches, both in oversight and as officiants at the Liturgy. As we shall see, this had a huge effect on the understanding of the presbyterate and the Liturgy.[26]

Christians were now able to share much more fully in public and social life.[27] This widening of interests had of course brought its dangers. For the prevailing notion of "civilized living" was at odds with Christianity in its customs and assumptions. It was inevitable that, as in the days of St Paul, Christians had to navigate their way through the ensuing dilemmas. But if the world was ever to be Christianized then the Church had to take on the risk of being secularized in the process. So life as a whole, social and political life as well as the personal conduct of individuals, began for the first time to feel the impact of the gospel and to be framed on Christian assumptions. The laws regarding women and children were made more gentle. Orphanages, hospitals and almshouses for the aged were set up—all unknown in the ancient world. The worst atrocities of the amphitheatre and the gladiatorial shows were abolished. Moreover, for the first time, political power was made accountable to God. Thus the emperor Theodosius was obliged to do penance as a Christian communicant for ordering a massacre at Thessalonica.[28] It underlined the salient point of the early Church's contention with the empire, for which the martyrs had given their lives: that the world and all in it are subject to the Lordship of Christ and the Kingdom of God.

This expansion of the faith into the whole of human life brought a flowering of Christian philosophy. As Dix puts it, just as the martyr had out-fought his persecutors, and the monk who had given his whole life to God had out-fought old assumptions about what life was for, so a constellation of Christian doctors and theologians, such as Basil, Jerome and Augustine, out-thought the exhausted tradition of philosophical speculation. They did this not by simply rejecting it, but by absorbing the very best of classical culture.²⁹

In these different ways, the Church revised its practice of worship and made its mark on the culture of its day. In 410, Rome was sacked by Alaric and his army of Goths, but by then the Mediterranean world was so far Christian that there was to be no going back.³⁰

Changes in the mediaeval period

In this section, I shall draw particularly on Paul F. Bradshaw and Maxwell E. Johnson's *The Eucharistic Liturgies*, whilst continuing to note Gregory Dix's interpretation.

In the year 800, Pope Gregory III crowned Charlemagne Holy Roman Emperor, in true succession to the Caesars. He had chosen him to restore order and Christianity to Western Europe. Charlemagne at once set about the preaching and teaching of the faith and imported the best scholars to guide him in this task. As most of his people were illiterate, the Liturgy was extremely important, as it was their entry-point into the drama of the central mysteries of Christianity. In 800, there were several different liturgical traditions in use throughout Western Europe. It was Charlemagne and his successors, rather than the Roman Church, who pressed for greater unity, and by the end of the Middle Ages the Roman rite was essentially *the* rite in the West.³¹

From then on until the eve of the Reformation, there were further significant changes in the Liturgy. It was filled out with numerous accretions, particularly within and around the great prayer of thanksgiving. This shift in balance is inseparable from the changes in the status and role of the priest in relation to the laity.

In the corporate worship of the early Church, the only part of the Liturgy which belonged exclusively to the bishop was the recitation of the thanksgiving prayer. The fraction and the administration of communion he shared with the presbyters and the deacons, and he had no special part in the offertory, which was performed by the laity. Beginning even in the fourth century there was the addition of many prayers around the thanksgiving prayer: a prayer at the fraction, a prayer over the people immediately before communion, a prayer of thanksgiving after the communion, and a final blessing. All these prayers and more were assigned to the celebrant alone. In later centuries (800–1100), there was a further accumulation of devotional extras around the various moments of the liturgical action. Again these accrued to the priest, and in many the wording was personal to him. The question was whether the earlier basic structure and meaning remained intact: the accent on the action, and the respective roles of the participants in that action.[32]

Beginning in the late fourth century in Syria, there had been a tendency for people not to receive communion every time they attended the Eucharist, and this trend spread over the centuries, first to Jerusalem and from there across the Eastern Church, and then also to the West. It was almost certainly connected with the growth of a devotional sense of fear and awe before the consecrated sacrament.[33] The biblical root was St Paul's warning that the Corinthian Christians were profaning the body and blood: "Any one who eats and drinks without discerning the body eats and drinks judgment upon himself" (1 Corinthians 11:29). For many, it seemed safer to restrict oneself most of the time to what became known as "spiritual communion". In the West in the twelfth century, this practice came to be justified by saying that it was union with God that was the ultimate purpose of the Eucharist, so that physical reception of the elements was not essential; some other devotional practice was just as effective for the believer's salvation.[34]

Moreover, the priest was now understood to receive communion on behalf of the people. Naturally those who did not receive communion ceased to bring gifts of bread and wine from home for the offertory. In any case, from the ninth century onwards, unleavened bread (to match the bread at the Last Supper) was specially prepared in monastic houses and began to replace the ordinary bread previously supplied by the laity. Moreover, separate individual wafers for communicants were baked, so that they no longer shared in a common loaf; the fraction thus lost its connection with the sharing of the one loaf and became tied to the breaking of Christ's body. Moreover, in order to avoid any spillage of the sacred elements, the wafers were placed on the tongue and not in the hands of worshippers, and increasingly reception was just of the bread. Because the words over the consecrated elements were considered the most sacred part of the rite, they came to be recited in a low voice, and later in silence. Thus laypeople could not hear the central part of the rite (which in any case was in Latin). Nor could they see what was happening on the altar, since by now the priest faced east. Moreover, the action at the high altar on Sunday Mass was partially screened off, and veiled entirely during Lent.[35]

It is easy to infer from all this that the laity were rendered passive and distant in the Eucharistic worship, even alienated from it. Certainly they were being encouraged to pursue their own devotions. Bradshaw and Johnson do refer to Eamon Duffy in *The Stripping of the Altars* to show that screens and veils were not intended to exclude, but to heighten the value of the spectacle temporarily concealed. They also draw attention to substitute participation of the laity through extra variable prayers of intercession in the vernacular and painted emblems (such as a crucifix) which were passed round the congregation for them to kiss, as a means of uniting individuals in a corporate body. Moreover, for those who could read there were various commentaries on the Mass, and these included allegorical interpretations of the Eucharist, where each facet was related to the life and death of Christ.[36] But much of the devotional material was quite separate from the Mass. This was clearly a rupture in the corporate action as understood in the early Church, and in the conviction, engrained in the early Church from Paul to Augustine and beyond, that "the body" referred both to the elements and to the Church: now it clearly referred overwhelmingly to the elements and scarcely to the members.

There was a further way in which the role and status of the priest were inflated: over the Eucharistic sacrifice and the "private" Mass. Even as early as Cyprian in the third century, there were those who believed that the clergy were the ones who offered *on behalf of* the laity. This eventually became a standard part of the Roman canon. The original wording at the commemoration of the living, "who offer you this sacrifice of praise" was prefixed by the alternative "for whom we offer". When this was used, it changed the men and women mentioned from being those who offer *themselves* to those *for whom* the Mass was offered by the priest. It was then a small step for the presence of any laypeople to be viewed as inconsequential, and so the way was opened for "private" masses.

The conferring of holy orders was now being defined primarily in terms of the power of celebrating the Eucharist, particularly seen as the power to sacrifice. Now deputizing for the bishop, one in each congregation, rather naturally they wanted to exercise their role fully. The practice grew of daily Eucharists. This raised the question of how that sacrifice related to the sacrifice by Christ on Calvary. Although almost all theologians continued to hold that the Mass was not a new sacrifice but a commemoration of the passion of Christ, in popular imagination it was an addition to or repetition of the sacrifice on Calvary. And the "fruits" of the Mass were thought of in a quantitative sense: the more the better. So masses proliferated. Low Mass was developed, which was normally said by just the officiant and one assistant. Moreover, the practice grew of celebrations for all kinds of special occasions. The laity presented alms and endowments to monasteries and churches, and the clergy would repay the generosity with offerings of the Eucharist for these benefactors. This was the root of mass-stipends. And when the benefactor is not present, the Eucharist becomes something which the priest inevitably does *for* the laity, not *with* them, even if they are with him in spirit and he does it at their request.[37]

Another factor which accentuated the status and role of the celebrant while threatening the role of the laity and the corporate nature of the rite was an increasing concern with the question of the consecration of the elements and the presence of Christ. At what precise point did the bread and wine become the body and blood of Christ? The early Church, with its intense concentration on the action as a single whole, had not even considered this question. Now the precise point of consecration became a thorny issue. Wherever it was determined to be (most likely at Christ's words of institution or the invocation of the Holy Spirit), it was certainly within the thanksgiving prayer, and that had the effect of attracting other prayers to be inserted within it. It was no doubt felt that they would be more effective by that close association. So a raft of intercessions was inserted after the point of consecration.[38]

This issue spawned long debates about the relationship between the physical body of Christ and what was received in the Eucharist. But it was also a practical question, because in the Middle Ages there emerged the practice of the priest elevating the bread during the narrative of institution in order to show it to the people for them to adore it. Gazing at the body of Christ and adoring it at the elevation became the devotional climax of the rite. People felt free to leave the Mass immediately, and they would dash from altar to altar to catch a glimpse of the consecrated host more than once.[39]

To summarize:

In all this we are getting near a divorce between the corporate offering and the priesthood of the priest. The priest is now seen to do the Eucharist simply in virtue of his personal possession of holy orders, without sufficient regard to the fact that the Eucharist is a corporate act of the Church, incomplete without the other "orders" in the organic body of Christ.

The offertory and the communion were the two active roles of the laity in what was a single action: the one who offered also communicated. Now the offertory had disappeared; and communion was rare. Dix dolefully notes that the layperson became a mere spectator and listener, without a "liturgy" in the primitive sense at all.[40]

The eschatological meaning of the Eucharist, which we repeatedly encountered earlier, had been almost completely lost. In the old rite, the participants had focussed on the whole person and work of Christ. The Church entered into his action as a unity, each performing their office within it, and so had become more and more what it eternally is: his body. In a similar way, the classical understanding of *anamnesis*, which I presented earlier, had been virtually reduced to individual meditation on the death of Christ.

This account of the loss of the classical understanding of the shape and content of the Liturgy has a strong affinity with the criticisms of mediaeval rationalizing of the tradition made by Henri de Lubac and the integralists: a philosophical schema was being substituted for the living God, and nature and supernature were being related in an extrinsic way.

On the eve of the Reformation what was needed was a thorough consideration of the whole tradition, and especially that of the Church of the first five centuries. But the materials necessary to do that were very limited at the time, and in any case the whole atmosphere was too febrile and fractious to encourage any such investigation.

The Reformation era: Archbishop Cranmer

Archbishop Thomas Cranmer entered fully into the debates of the continental Reformers. After the death of Henry VIII in 1547 and the accession of boy king Edward VI, he drew on all his liturgical skills to produce first the 1549 *Book of Common Prayer*, and then the more radical version of 1552. In both, there was a heavy emphasis on the sacrifice of Christ "once offered" on the cross. The rite itself was a commemoration of that sacrifice, a sacrifice of prayer and thanksgiving. No other sense of sacrifice was admitted, and in the 1552 version even the idea of offering "ourselves, our souls, and bodies" was removed from the canon and included only in an optional prayer after communion. The whole prayer was focussed on thanksgiving, in line with the Eucharistic Prayers of the early Church; in the 1552 version, the faithful were urged to eat and drink in remembrance of Christ's death with thanksgiving. (In this section, I draw not only on Dix but also on William R. Crockett's chapter "Holy Communion" in *The Study of Anglicanism*, edited by Stephen Sykes and John Booty (1988), pp. 272–85, and his book *Eucharist: Symbol of Transformation* (1989).)

Gregory Dix was very critical of Cranmer, believing that he used his skills as a liturgist to fill old words with a quite different meaning: gone was the objective presence of Christ in the elements, and the emphasis was really on the individual and the subjective feelings of the worshippers, their inner conviction and earnest emotions. He lamented that it was as if devotionally the mediaeval layman's independent meditation on the Passion at the Mass had actually become the Liturgy and Eucharistic action itself.[41] He believed that the classical shape and substance had been lost. Yet Cranmer was not denying the real presence of Christ. His aim was to reunite consecration with communion, so that Christ was not present as an object on the altar to be adored, but as spiritual food and drink to nourish the faith of believers. Consecration is seen as the setting apart for the sacred use of communion. The elements are instrumental in communicating the presence of Christ to the faithful receiver. So the approach is not purely subjective but personalist, with a real participation in Christ.[42]

This position is known as "receptionism". It takes for granted the real presence but relates it primarily to the faithful communicant rather than to the elements of bread and wine. Richard Hooker, who developed the doctrine, wrote, "Let it therefore be sufficient for me presenting myself at the Lord's table to know what there I receive from him, without searching or inquiring into the manner how Christ performeth his promise ... It is enough that to me ... [the elements] are the body and blood of Christ." Hooker's words reflect the emerging Anglican tradition that nothing can be proposed as a necessary article of faith which goes beyond the certain testimony of Scripture.[43]

This development connects with another factor influencing Cranmer's thinking. He was very conscious of the need for national unity at a time of great upheaval and dissension. His chosen route was the Royal Supremacy, whereby Church and nation were a single entity under a godly monarch. Political power was allied with liturgical uniformity, and it made sense to have a liturgy which was light on doctrine.

Dix was surely right to be highly critical of the Royal Supremacy, in that the monarch controlled the Church through Parliament for 400 years. This was an all too implausible resolution of Christ's injunction to render to Caesar the things that are Caesar's and to God the things that are God's. It also blotted out St Peter's question to the Jewish authorities, whether it was right in the sight of God to listen to them rather than to God (Acts 4:19). And the early Church had tenaciously fought the Roman empire precisely to uphold the conviction that the state could not demand unconditional obedience to the emperor.[44]

Moreover, though Dix is mistaken to claim that Cranmer's liturgy is purely subjectivist, he is justified in asking whether proper attention was given to the relation of the elements to the person of Christ. William Crockett in *Eucharist: Symbol of Transformation* perceptively proposes that there was a fundamental inconsistency, not to say incoherence, in Cranmer's sacramental theology. Cranmer was a realist in his understanding of the Incarnation, life, death and resurrection of Christ, and in affirming a real union and mutual indwelling between Christ and Christian believers. Here he shows his biblical and patristic roots. But he was influenced by late mediaeval philosophical ideas known as nominalism which dissolved the unity of symbol and reality. For

Cranmer, the body of Christ is present only in heaven, so in logic it followed that it cannot also be on earth associated with the elements (this is evident in the rubrics). In this, he agreed with the Swiss Reformers over against Luther. He does believe in the reality of the sacramental gift in the Eucharist, but it has to be related to reception by faith and not to the elements.[45]

So Cranmer rightly re-emphasized thankful communion, but he imperilled the connection between the signs of bread and wine and the reality in which they participated. The danger was that the Eucharist would be seen as just one means of grace in the worship of the Church, and not its central act. Moreover, his rite lays great emphasis on worthy reception by the individual, whereas acknowledgement of the Church as "the mystical body of thy Son, which is the blessed company of all faithful people" appears only in an optional prayer at the end of the Communion service.

Widening interpretation

In spite of the rigidities of the Act of Uniformity, which heads the contents of the *Book of Common Prayer*, room was found for a diversity of interpretation. This was first of all because the Elizabethan Prayer Book of 1559 assured communicants that they were receiving the body and blood of Christ. Moreover, the Convocation of bishops affirmed that Christ really is present under the kinds of bread and wine, and that after consecration the substance is the body and blood of Christ. In the seventeenth century, there was renewed study of the Church Fathers, and through it there began the broadening of the senses in which the Eucharist is a sacrifice. Without in any way undermining the "once-for-all" character of Christ's sacrifice on Calvary, the Church was also seen to offer itself in union with Christ, its head.[46]

In the eighteenth century, we have the Evangelical Revival of John and Charles Wesley. This was as much a Eucharistic revival as an Evangelical one. For they saw the unity of a sacramental and an Evangelical vision of Christianity. This is evident in the collection of 166 Eucharistic hymns they composed, prefaced by an extract from a treatise by Daniel Brevint,

The Christian Sacrament and Sacrifice, from the seventeenth century. Brevint saw the Eucharist as having a past, present and future aspect. It is a memorial of the saving death of Christ; it is present grace and nourishment for worthy receivers; and it is also a pledge which assures believers of their participation in the life of the promised Kingdom of God. Brevint affirmed not only that the Eucharist is a commemorative sacrifice and also a sacrifice of the Church in union with its Head; he added that Christ is the eternal High Priest who continually presents his completed sacrifice before the Father in heaven as the basis for the acceptance of believers.[47]

The Oxford Movement of the nineteenth century emphasized the catholic inheritance of Anglicanism, insisting on the sacramental life and on the Eucharist as the centre of catholic worship. It saw a closer connection than the earlier Anglican tradition between the real presence of Christ in the Eucharist and the elements, by affirming a strict identity between the earthly body of Christ, his risen body, and his sacramental body: there is one Lord Jesus Christ; the only difference is the mode of his presence. Christ is certainly not present in the Eucharist in a physical mode, but by means of sacramental signs. The presence of Christ in relation to the elements is brought about by the act of consecration and is not dependent on their reception in communion. Christ is indeed objectively present in relation to the elements but present in grace only to those who receive him by faith.[48] The Oxford Movement also asserted the essential independence of the Church from the state against the Royal Supremacy and stressed the social mission of the Church against any narrowing of it to individual conversion and morality. This was the tradition which Gregory Dix inhabited and from which he assessed Cranmer's work.

Meanwhile, a thorough consideration of the whole tradition, and especially that of the Church of the first four centuries, was underway. Starting in a French monastery in 1875, the Liturgical Movement came to acquire international importance. It was a sustained search for the renewal of liturgical understanding. At first, it was rather focussed on the past, but it reinvigorated study of the Liturgy and its continual importance for the life of the Church and the world. Along with the integralist approach it bore fruit in the Second Vatican Council (1962–5) and its documents.

Indeed, there has been a convergence of liturgies among the different churches. The Iona Community is one very important centre. Through the inspiration of George MacLeod, it revived the Celtic tradition of St Columba and revitalized the Church's engagement with life in society in all its aspects, starting with the industrialization and poverty of Glasgow in the 1930s. Several fine English scholars and priests made significant contributions to the Movement, including Gabriel Hebert with his *Liturgy and Society* and *Parish Communion: A Book of Essays*, which he edited; the most notable of these was Gregory Dix (see *The Shape of the Liturgy*, pp. 250f. and 752 for his linking of Liturgy and social-political issues). In the second half of the twentieth century, the Church of England at last became free to conduct extended experimentation with its Liturgy, and as the new millennium dawned, it produced its own *Common Worship*.

Finally, the Ecumenical Movement and ecumenical scholarship have been very influential. These include the Anglican-Roman Catholic *Agreed Statement on Eucharistic Doctrine*, and the World Council of Churches document *Baptism, Eucharist and Ministry*. The first acknowledges that the goal of the Eucharist is communion with Christ, which presupposes his true presence. It is effectively signified by the bread and wine, which in this mystery become his body and blood. The presence of Christ does not depend on the individual's faith in order to be the Lord's real gift to the Church, but it is only through reception by faith that a life-giving encounter results. The same document affirms the view of *anamnesis* held by the early Church: the Eucharistic memorial is the effectual proclamation in the present of the once-for-all event of the past, since the sacrifice of the cross is made sacramentally present in order that believers may participate here and now in its redemptive reality.

The WCC document stresses the celebratory character of the Eucharist: it is a communal act of praise and thanksgiving for the whole sweep of creation and redemption, in contrast to the intense focus on the death of Christ and the penitential note running through Cranmer's liturgy. The Eucharist is not only an act of personal communion, but a corporate community celebration in which all the participants are built up into communion with Christ and with one another in the body of Christ. Furthermore, the role of the Holy Spirit in the celebration, long recognized by the Eastern Orthodox churches, is reflected in the restoration of the invocation of the Holy Spirit (*epiklesis*). The whole rite is an anticipation of the meal prepared in the Kingdom of God. This contributes to the restoration of the eschatological perspective visible in the earliest Eucharistic traditions in the New Testament. And this in turn is linked to the pursuit of justice in this world. For the vision of a meal in the completed Kingdom of God challenges the status quo in society and the prevailing set of economic and social relations.[49]

This chapter has set out the historical development of the shape, content and understanding of the Liturgy, particularly the roots in the first five centuries, and showed the modern recovery of their importance. It has also indicated at various points their fit with the integralist approach described at the end of Part 2.

The next Part will spell out more fully a version of the Christian faith, in a study of the magisterial ecumenical work of Rowan Williams, who stands in close continuity with Gregory Dix and develops his own integralist approach.

Notes

[1] Peter Frankopan, *The Silk Roads: A New History of the World*, p. 54.
[2] *Didache*, ix. 4, in Dix's translation, *The Shape of the Liturgy*, p. 90; Paul F. Bradshaw and Maxwell E. Johnson, *The Eucharistic Liturgies: Their Evolution and Interpretation*, pp. 14–16.
[3] Gregory Dix, *The Shape of the Liturgy*, pp. 1f., 12, 35.
[4] Dix, *The Shape of the Liturgy*, pp. 48–50.
[5] Dix, *The Shape of the Liturgy*, pp. 55–78, 141.
[6] Dix, *The Shape of the Liturgy*, pp. 243–55; the quotations from Augustine are on p. 247.
[7] Bradshaw and Johnson, *The Eucharistic Liturgies*, pp. 20–4.
[8] Bradshaw and Johnson, *The Eucharistic Liturgies*, pp. 53f.
[9] Dix, *The Shape of the Liturgy*, pp. 141–54.
[10] Dix, *The Shape of the Liturgy*, pp. 304f., 320.
[11] Dix, *The Shape of the Liturgy*, p. 307.
[12] Dix, *The Shape of the Liturgy*, pp. 331, 305, 318.

13 Dix, *The Shape of the Liturgy*, p. 305.
14 Dix, *The Shape of the Liturgy*, pp. 151, 143, 323f.
15 Dix, *The Shape of the Liturgy*, pp. 320–3.
16 Dix, *The Shape of the Liturgy*, pp. 327f.
17 Bradshaw and Johnson, *The Eucharistic Liturgies*, p. 71.
18 Dix, *The Shape of the Liturgy*, pp. 328f.
19 Bradshaw and Johnson, *The Eucharistic Liturgies*, pp. 69f., 74, 64.
20 Dix, *The Shape of the Liturgy*, p. 304.
21 Dix, *The Shape of the Liturgy*, p. 336.
22 Dix, *The Shape of the Liturgy*, pp. 337–41.
23 Dix, *The Shape of the Liturgy*, pp. 343–6, 333.
24 Dix, *The Shape of the Liturgy*, pp. 306–14.
25 Dix, *The Shape of the Liturgy*, pp. 312f., 315, 382.
26 Dix, *The Shape of the Liturgy*, p. 310.
27 Dix, *The Shape of the Liturgy*, p. 307.
28 Dix, *The Shape of the Liturgy*, pp. 387f.
29 Dix, *The Shape of the Liturgy*, p. 392.
30 Dix, *The Shape of the Liturgy*, p. 496.
31 Bradshaw and Johnson, *The Eucharistic Liturgies*, pp. 193f.
32 Dix, *The Shape of the Liturgy*, pp. 318f., 522–5.
33 Dix, *The Shape of the Liturgy*, pp. 594, 442, 436.
34 Bradshaw and Johnson, *The Eucharistic Liturgies*, pp. 210f.
35 Bradshaw and Johnson, *The Eucharistic Liturgies*, pp. 211–14.
36 Bradshaw and Johnson, *The Eucharistic Liturgies*, pp. 214–18.
37 Bradshaw and Johnson, *The Eucharistic Liturgies*, pp. 218–21; Dix, *The Shape of the Liturgy*, pp. 593f.
38 Dix, *The Shape of the Liturgy*, pp. 437, 442, 598.
39 Bradshaw and Johnson, *The Eucharistic Liturgies*, pp. 222–30.
40 Dix, *The Shape of the Liturgy*, pp. 318f., 436, 598.
41 Dix, *The Shape of the Liturgy*, pp. 648–56.
42 William R. Crockett, "Holy Communion", in Sykes, Stephen and Booty, John (eds), *The Study of Anglicanism*, pp. 272–85, here at 273–7.
43 Crockett, "Holy Communion", pp. 274f.
44 Dix, *The Shape of the Liturgy*, pp. 654, 679f.
45 William R. Crockett, *Eucharist: Symbol of Transformation*, pp. 167–70.

46 Dix, *The Shape of the Liturgy*, pp. 674f.; Crockett, "Holy Communion", p. 276.
47 Crockett, "Holy Communion", pp. 277f.
48 Crockett, "Holy Communion", pp. 278f.
49 Crockett, "Holy Communion", pp. 279–82.

PART 4

The Faith

In his Foreword to editor Simon Jones' *The Sacramental Life: Gregory Dix and his Writings*, Rowan Williams writes,

> *The Shape of the Liturgy* offers a shape for the whole of Christian thinking. Its central image is the single movement of the Son to the Father, in eternity and in time, the outpouring of the Son to the Father in the Trinity... Within this divine movement, God's journey into God, we find our life and our hope, the judgment of all we are and have been, the gift that renews us and transforms every relation, social and personal, so that we can speak, in Dix's wonderful phrase, of *homo eucharisticus*, the renewed human species that is defined in and through the Eucharist... The whole book evokes as few others do a sense of what it is simply to inhabit the Christian universe, a world centred upon the Word made flesh.[1]

In *Christ the Heart of Creation*, Rowan Williams emphasizes that there is an intrinsic connection between devotion and reflection. Our practices of worship and devotion—for example, singing hymns and bowing before an icon of the Saviour—press upon us the question of how we speak both *about* Jesus and *to* him. Conversely, if this speaking develops and matures, in turn it generates a deeper and steadier devotion—and, I would add, a more faithful practice in the world. In this way, Christ is never a passive object to be discussed, but continues to put in question and to transfigure the lives of those who acknowledge him as the eternal Word made flesh.

Williams aims to clarify how the Church's language about Jesus works. This is no abstruse matter. Increased clarity can lead to increased credibility, not as the conclusion of an argument but because it would offer a coherent context for human living. It would give more depth and substance to imagining what it is like to believe and what new connections and possibilities are opened up.

How are we to think about the relation between God and what God has made?

> If God is truly the source, the ground and the context of every limited, finite state of affairs, if God is the action or agency that makes everything else active, then God cannot be spoken of as one item in a list of the forces active in the world. God's action cannot be added to the action of some other agent in order to make a more effective force. And this also means that God's action is never in *competition* with any particular activity inside the universe ... [D]ivine and created action could never stand alongside each other as rivals (so that the more there is of one, the less there would be of the other). God makes the world to be *itself*, to have an integrity and completeness and goodness that is—by God's gift—its own. At the same time, God makes the world to be open to a relation with God's own infinite life that can enlarge and transfigure the created order without destroying it.

All this is summed up

> in a Christ who is uninterruptedly living a creaturely, finite life on earth and at the same time living out of the depths of divine life and uninterruptedly enjoying the relation that eternally subsists between the divine Source or Father and the divine Word or Son. It is in this sense that we can rightly speak of Jesus as *the heart of creation*, the one on whom all the patterns of finite existence converge to find their meaning.

So the book attempts to trace something of the mutual illumination that connects the doctrine of Christ (Christology) with the doctrine of creation. God and the world are not two things to be added together: it is a case of non-duality. Neither are they two things that are "really" one thing: it is a case of non-identity. They stand in an asymmetrical relation, in which the world depends wholly on God, yet is fully itself, made to be and to act according to its own logic and structure.[2]

This is Rowan Williams' version of an integralist approach, worked out ecumenically in dialogue with a host of conversation partners across the ages, Orthodox, Catholic and Protestant. He particularly acknowledges his debt to the distinguished Anglican theologian Austin Farrer (1904–68), but the basic ideas lie deep in the tradition.

At the heart of Rowan Williams' vision is his concern to proclaim the good news of God's utterly gracious, utterly gratuitous love. If his wording is often difficult, that is because the good news not only offers profound reassurance but also confronts us with a disturbing challenge. For it poses to me the practical question of what difference it is going to make to my life. And since it is offered indiscriminately to everyone on the planet, it asks what difference it is going to make to the way we relate to each other in a common life. To believe and act upon such good news would be very difficult indeed. Yet Williams insists that if we do not hear the challenge, we have not heard the gospel.[3] Let us start, then, by considering God and creation.

God and creation

God just *is*—uncreated, eternal. God is entirely free to be God. God has no needs at all. Therefore there was no need for God to create the universe. God is pure gift, and the universe is the "overflow" of God's love and life. God freely desires to be God for what is not God—desires the flourishing of what is not God. God is always supremely there with the world and for the world, granting it meaning and worth. Everything is therefore utterly dependent on God for its existence.[4]

In Genesis 1, there is just a hint that when God created the world there was some primordial chaotic material on which God had to work to make an orderly cosmos. But the overwhelming impression is that God had only to say the word and things were created. This is reinforced in

Second Isaiah (40–55). Again there is the story of how in the days of old God cut the dragon of chaos in pieces (Isaiah 51:9). But this is utterly outweighed by passages such as 40:26 and 48:13, where God creates effortlessly, bringing out the hosts of stars by number and calling them by name. There is no struggle with any other power. There is just the free utterance of the One who is the initiating agency of all. That is what is meant by "creation from nothing" (*creatio ex nihilo*). Why is there anything at all? Relate everything fundamentally to God the Creator.[5]

Human beings are seen as the crown of creation. They are "in the image of God" (Genesis 1:26; cf. Psalm 8). The West has a long history of identifying the particular human features meant by this phrase, especially the power of reason. It is probably wiser to say that it points to humans being persons capable of having communion with God, who is consistently portrayed in at least personal terms.

In the Hebrew tradition, humans are thought of as a unity of spirit, soul and flesh (*ruach, nephesh, basar*). This non-dualistic outlook is endorsed in the New Testament: it hails the resurrection of the body, not the immortality of the soul. So in 1 Corinthians 15:44, Paul says we are a physical body in this life, and we shall be a spiritual body in the next. This was at odds with the typical Greek understanding, where there is a dualism between eternal and temporal, mind and matter, soul and body. Thus Paul encountered trouble at Athens when he spoke of Christ's resurrection from the dead (Acts 17:31f.).

As it pursued its missionary expansion the Church had to wrestle with the relation of Hebrew and Greek idioms. The prologue to St John's Gospel is an early sign of this: "In the beginning was the *Logos*". *Logos* means "word", but also "reason" and "structure"—hence "logic" and "logistics". The Greek Father St Maximus the Confessor (580–662) worked with the Hebrew belief that this world of time and space is "very good" (Genesis 1:31) and took up the notion of the eternal *Logos*. This is expressed in the orderliness of creation as a *cosmos*, so that every finite creature has its own *logos*, and thus participates in the life of the eternal *Logos*.[6]

Maximus also drew on ideas stemming from the Greek philosopher Aristotle (384–322 BC), who as a biologist was conscious that organisms develop through time to full maturity. Maximus believed that the *logos* of any creature is an inner principle (we'd perhaps say DNA) shaping the activity of creatures to their full and final actualization. *Logos* thus has a dynamic forward-looking sense. This was contrary to the prevalent Greek idea that life moved in endless circles; or, more pessimistically, that life had fallen from its ideal spiritual *logos*, and that the body was a tomb (*soma sema*) from which it needed to escape to its original world. By contrast, Maximus believed that history moves towards a goal. And he believed that the more a creature moves towards its full actualization, the closer it is to the Creator.[7]

Greek philosophers had tended to believe that any God would be one and static. They were bothered by a world of multiplicity and change, and inclined to deny any involvement of God in it. However, Maximus recognized the sheer diversity of the created order, and believed that if it acted as it should, it would then become a harmonious unity-in-diversity, reflecting the life lived by the eternal *Logos*. So all finite creatures needed to be fully aligned with their own *logos*, and so exist in an optimal relation with the eternal *Logos*.[8]

In this process, Maximus believed that humans were unique in two ways. First he distinguished human nature and human agency. All humans have a common nature, that is, the *kind* of creatures they are. But that nature does not exist in some higher world: it is found only in particular human beings, who are agents, with their particular and unrepeatable performance within the world, marked by their choices and acts. Secondly, being in the image of God, they are not just natural exactly like other creatures. They have the freedom to be actively engaged in harmonizing the whole created order, as part of their "liturgical" service to God.[9] A biblical root of this lies in Romans 12:1–2: "I appeal to you therefore ... by the mercies of God, to present your bodies as a living sacrifice, holy and acceptable to God, which is your spiritual worship. Do not be conformed to this world but be transformed by the renewal of your mind." There is an intrinsic relation between the restoration of the integrity of the person and the transformation of the world. Worship and life are inseparable. The Greek for "spiritual worship" is *logike latreia*. *Logike* means "belonging to the *logos*"—the *logos* of the whole person, not spirit separated from mind and body. *Latreia* is an equivalent of *leitourgia*.

The Fall

In the story told in Genesis 1-2, God graciously provides for the man and the woman all that makes for a pleasant and harmonious life: the rhythms of nature, food from many sources, water in abundance, the garden to till and maintain; the companionship and union of man and woman, the invitation to be fruitful and multiply. They live in a state of timeless innocence. Yet perversely a malign force prompts suspicion (Genesis 3). The serpent insinuates that God is a deceiver, holding back something to which Adam and Eve are entitled: the knowledge of good and evil. It is presumably knowledge which empowers humans to make their way in the world and create cultures. It is clearly not bad in itself; but it can and will be used as a desirable defence against a God who is presumed jealously to hoard power. The consequence is the loss of innocence: mutual recrimination and rupture in the relation between man and woman, so that companionship turns into male rule; pain in childbirth and toil in making a living are multiplied; and nature becomes an alien battlefield. The authors plainly see the root of all this in the suspicion or neglect of God, the desire to be in control, to be as gods ourselves. The prospect of unending life is forfeited, and all that awaits at the last is dusty death (yes, Shakespeare's *Macbeth* is a tale of "vaulting ambition" overleaping the confines of time).

Adam and Eve are every man and every woman. And the story is plainly about the exercise of power and the issue of God: whether God is, and if so, what sort of God. Much that human beings do in the exercise of their powers is humane and constructive. But mixed in with that is the perverse self-interested use of power. There has been plenty of it in recent times: false economic ideas and reckless ambition combined to make the economic system implode in 2008; the direst warnings about climate change are repudiated by those whose financial ambitions are challenged; and we have a resurgence of alpha males asserting their dominance, both domestically and on an international scale. It suddenly turns out that the quaint story of the Tower of Babel (Genesis 11:1-9) unpacks much insight: men use the latest technology to build a skyscraper and make a name for themselves. It is a tale of boundless ambition for a security shield which would be a final defence against the threat of the "other".[10]

There is nothing wrong with power itself. Humans are active beings and need the capacity to get things done. However, power is never an abstract matter, but extremely practical, and demands the question of how it is to be used. In the West, we lay great emphasis on the individual. We say we need to realize ourselves. We invent and reinvent ourselves. But we also know that others are bent on realizing themselves, and we fear being conscripted into somebody else's agenda. So we have to assert ourselves, to be in control. Life becomes an endless battle of power games, as we anxiously negotiate our way through life.[11] So we come to treat competition, exclusion, insecurity and violence as necessary and normal.[12]

The only sane way is surely to drop the initial idea that I am born an individual and then move out to relate to others. From start to finish, we are who we are *in relation*. We have first to think of ourselves as existing with others and for others. In our culture, this comes far more easily to women than to men. But our goal of a harmonious and peaceful world is elusive. We surely also need to go back to what we said about God as pure gift, and the world as an overflow of the divine love and life, where God freely desires the flourishing of God's good creation. So our utter dependence on this kind of God should prompt not suspicion but trust. For God is not another item in the universe which is a potential threat to my security. God does not have to construct or negotiate an identity. God is entirely free to be God without any process of struggle. God alone is beyond the precarious exchanges of needy creatures. Rowan Williams concludes that properly understood, this is the most liberating affirmation we could ever hear.[13]

So it becomes clear that really, the God we suspect is just a projection. It is a projection of human notions of what an absolutely powerful God would be like—a crippling and deadly fantasy, rooted in fear. But it is one that is so deeply engrained that it spawns endless cycles of strife and violence. It is particularly prone to flare up in religious settings, where one group will confront another in the name of God, who has supposedly provided them with the sure and certain data to warrant their actions. The history of Israel is one of perversity: of continually jeopardizing the covenant given by God, in which the promise is that God shall be their God. The people are wayward in the desert wanderings, and kingship is experienced as profoundly ambiguous, with a tendency of the kings to seduction by the gods of Canaan and the temptations of wealth and power. The life of a prophet is often lonely and doomed to failure and even death. Nathan risked his life to confront David with his conduct towards Uriah and Bathsheba. This does not cease with the experience of the exile to Babylon or the restoration to the Promised Land and the emergence of Judaism. It is a mercy that the Jews did not suppress but preserved the memory of perversity in their scriptures. The hope was born that this perversity would finally be overcome by God's initiative.

The road to the cross

William Temple wrote:

> God has made the world; that was quite easy; but now He must enter into the lowest depths of the experience which the created world made possible, in order that He might interpenetrate it all and fill it with Himself; that it might be truly His, which was the purpose of making it, He must utterly give Himself to it. This is the unique point in Christian theology.[14]

The climax of all four Gospel narratives is the crucifixion of Jesus. Its shadow is cast back through the account of his ministry. The infancy narratives in Matthew and Luke already show the vulnerability of Jesus and foresee his death. Already in John's prologue, we know that the *Logos* came to his own, and his own people did not receive him. In Luke's Gospel, we are not halfway through when Jesus sets his face to go to Jerusalem, where he is to be taken up (9:51).

In *Christ the Heart of Creation*, Rowan Williams draws on the insights of Dietrich Bonhoeffer, recorded on his own road to martyrdom by the Nazis in 1945. One vital Reformation principle is that Jesus Christ in his Person and work must be understood as radically and entirely *for us*. Now if God is wholly for us in Christ (cf. Romans 8:31–9), then God is never seeking to displace our createdness in order to win a space for God in the world. Rather the challenge to us is to see in the incarnate Christ

God working towards the wholesale pervading of created reality by the divine without any loss of its integrity. This is Bonhoeffer's distinctive version of a non-competitive vision of finite and infinite.[15]

Bound up with this is the Reformation insistence on God's absolute freedom to be Jesus Christ. God cannot be constrained to act by the initiative of any creature.[16] This is played out in the Gospel story. First, in the temptations (Matthew 4:1-11; Luke 4:1-13), Jesus is tempted in three different ways to use power for worldly ends; in each case, he displays filial obedience to God. To act as God's full presence with us and for us, he upholds the complete trustworthiness of God. During his ministry he calls people to discipleship with his message of loving acceptance. He does not seek or defend any space for himself but gives himself without limit for the sake of the flourishing of others, stepping past ritual and all kinds of social boundaries to call men and women his brothers and sisters and friends. He draws the marginalized back into full membership, touching those who are unclean and eating with all and sundry. He attacks the Jewish leaders whose regulations set up barriers against access to God.[17] For undermining these divisions and exclusions he quickly encounters opposition from the Jewish authorities. They call for signs, but only dispute the signs he does perform. They seek every way of discrediting him and persuade themselves that he is an imposter. They take counsel regarding how to destroy him, and eventually succeed, through the betrayal by Judas.

In all this, their suspicions are confirmed at every turn. They know from their scriptures and traditions who their God is: a God of overwhelming power, waiting to bring in his Kingdom if only everyone obeys the Law. Every year, they celebrate their escape from Egypt and the gift of the land and pray for the peaceful possession of it under God, freed from their enemies. Jesus patently does not fulfil these assumptions. So they are constantly at loggerheads with him, and the more their alarm increases, the more they are determined to control the narrative and the situation.

In John's Gospel, the raising of Lazarus from death to life is intolerable. The chief priests and Pharisees gather in council, terrified that if they do not act decisively to stop Jesus, the Romans will come and destroy their temple and their nation. Caiaphas the High Priest tells them, "You know nothing at all; you do not understand that it is expedient for you that one man should die for the people." John goes on: "He did not say this of his own accord, but being high priest that year he prophesied that Jesus should die for the nation, and not for the nation only, but to gather into one the children of God who are scattered abroad" (John 11:47–52). When at the last they have him in their control, they perfect it by manoeuvring Pontius Pilate into sanctioning crucifixion—the most degrading and torturous punishment known.

Yet it is always God who is in control, and by his complete obedience Jesus displays God's authority at every stage of his ministry, and supremely in his final hours. He repeatedly outwits his detractors, subjecting them to questions they dare not answer. Of course he cannot ever win an argument to prove his case. For Jesus' authority depends on his wholly embodying what is being communicated: he is entirely an act of communication, an incarnate word. He *is* what he teaches. It is an authority of complete integrity, stemming from complete fidelity to his Father, which cannot be seen as derived from anything in the world external to him. It is a freedom which is finally revealed in complete immobility.[18]

At the Last Supper, loving his own to the end and foreseeing his betrayal and death, he anticipates them by giving new meaning to the bread and the cup, and commanding his followers, "Do this in remembrance of me." His farewell discourse encourages them not to be afraid, and he gives them his peace, which is not the peace that the world can offer. At the last, he triumphantly declares, "*Tetelestai*"—his work is done.

Just as the opponents of Jesus judge him by their own assumptions, so we try all kinds of gambits to evade his challenge. Bonhoeffer was a sworn foe of speculative questioning. Confident of our knowledge of good and evil, we love to construct a "map" of reality from our own standpoint. But that is to evade actual encounter with Christ. Who is it that I confront when I look at Jesus? To answer that question, we are tempted to select an identity for him. Here Williams reaches for the language of *logos* again. We find the roles are reversed. We find ourselves judged, and forced to ask, "Who am I?"—the title of a poem by Bonhoeffer himself. Encounter with Christ thus threatens human *logos* at the most fundamental level. My own *logos* is revealed as limited, so my life discovers its limit. Indeed the very fact of encounter with Christ establishes his right to ask us who we are—and so establishes who he is as divine *Logos*. For where Jesus is present, we have always already been met and judged and called to account. The human *logos* recognizes its true destiny only when its reasoning is interrupted and it is confronted with what demands its death. Faced with the radical challenge to its own *logos*, the human being must either die or kill Jesus.[19]

The trouble is that we humans tend to think of the divine as overwhelming power. But that will not recreate us, so that we are born again; it will not require the death of our *logos*. What is required is no less than a radically different understanding of God, one borne in on us by Christ's own life and death.[20]

It is common in Anglican circles to suppose that the focus of the self-emptying (*kenosis*) of the divine *Logos* in Jesus Christ lies in the Incarnation. This is inferred from the great hymn in Philippians (2:5–11). It is supposed that in the Incarnation certain divine attributes, such as omniscience and omnipotence, were suspended. No, says Bonhoeffer, the focus is the specific human humiliation of the cross, the rejection of Jesus as a sinner and a criminal. So it is not that *humanity* or even *finitude* as such conceals God. It is the suffering and failure and ambiguity of *this* particular human being that is the issue, the fact that God exists not only in him but as him. Bonhoeffer concentrates on his cumulative self-emptying. The *kenosis* involved in the Incarnation is not the taking on of human nature by a kind of metaphysical surgery. It is rather the living out of a humiliated and vulnerable life, and the scandal and the stumbling-block is a humanity in solidarity with those who are most powerless and apparently distant from God. God is intrinsically in this humble form: our liberation from sin and untruth is effected only by the act of unconditional love, which can be manifest only as a total renunciation of power or advantage:

> The freedom of the divine *Logos* is supremely active, supremely itself, in being embodied as the entirety of a human subject, uninterrupted in its humanness ... And in the particular vulnerability of this humanness—rejected and killed—the Word abandons any resort to proof or force and renounces any

> possibility of external confirmation to endorse its divine authority
> ... Christ is who he is as the one who exists for my and our sake.
> If Christ for a moment sought to coerce my response, that would
> mean that he ceased to be "for me" in this radical sense; he would
> be seeking to implement his will as a rival to mine, *and this is
> precisely what he has forgone in becoming human.*[21]

So I cannot think about Christ except as involved with me. This does not in any way imply an individualistic perspective. On the contrary, it puts my selfhood in question at its very foundation. My *logos* cannot live with Christ. This does not mean that there is a competition between me and Christ. The truth is really the opposite. My refusal to live in the presence of and for the sake of the other is a poisonous fiction: it exists only in our fearful imaginations. What must die in the encounter with Christ is *not* our finitude or createdness, but the delusion that we can live in denial of our finitude, our dependency on God as infinite agency.[22]

It is therefore Christ himself who creates the conditions for knowing him. It is only when we are judged by this *Logos* that our own old *logos* can learn anew its proper scope and limits and receive them. This is the only way in which we can tell the truth about finite reality: it is Christ who establishes the integrity and reality of finite existence. In the life of faith, we are radically directed towards the other and must be constantly willing to live under the questioning of the divine *Logos*. In this way, our finitude is affirmed, and we receive the promise that it will be glorified by grace.[23] (Cf. John 12:23–32: "The hour has come for the Son of man to be glorified... Now is my soul troubled. And what shall I say? 'Father, save me from this hour'? No, for this purpose I have come to this hour. Father, glorify thy name... Now is the judgment of this world, now shall the ruler of this world be cast out; and I, when I am lifted up from the earth, will draw all men to myself.")

This account helps to clarify the meaning of "freedom from constraint", by relating it to "freedom to be fully human", and it reveals that such freedom is fundamentally gifted to us. The cross surely radically calls in question the idea that we can confidently look to the unfolding of the possibilities inherent in creation for the resolution of our predicament. As

William Temple put it, human perversity brings infinite cost, not simply to us humans but to the heart of God.[24]

The resurrection

So we should not look for divine intervention of overwhelming power. We have seen that Jesus Christ enacts the emptying of power, the humiliation and the immobilization of the cross. His life is shown to be divine by utterly refusing what we might be tempted to regard as signs of divinity. In a similar way, the resurrection is not a triumphant epiphany or revelation of divine power so much as the bare impossibility of defeating and extinguishing the divine presence in Jesus: *as* the incarnate and crucified, he lives (cf. Peter's words at Acts 2:24).

This implies that the life and wellbeing of the creation cannot be found in the disruption of the finite world by some insertion of the infinite. On the contrary, Christ as finite, as creature, guarantees the integrity of the created order. Moreover, this finite—and more specifically mortal and suffering—Jesus releases into the world the act of the Creator, in new forms of relation and possibility. In this way, he makes it clear once and for all that it is only by bringing the Son's filial relationship into this finite world that creation's wholeness and fulfilment are realized.[25]

This takes us on to two topics: in one direction the Incarnation and the Trinity; in the other direction the Church. We shall see their integral relationship.

Incarnation and Trinity

We need first to see how Rowan Williams interprets the doctrines of the Incarnation and Trinity. It took centuries for the Church to draw out the implications of the event of Jesus Christ. Many proposals were tried and found wanting. To us the discussions can seem abstruse, but the acid test was whether they made sense of the Church's experience of living in response to Jesus Christ.

A major turning point was the Council of Nicaea in 325. Arius had a strong following for his attempt to fuse Graeco-Roman assumptions with the Christian faith, by proposing that Christ was not God but a demi-god, intermediate between God and the world. Rowan Williams sees in the controversy a contest over the relationship between God's power and God's love. Arius was so concerned to protect God's mysterious, unknowable transcendence and omnipotence that he proposed a God who cannot be known as the God of the Gospel, a Father who is wholly loving. Arius' God is entirely unconnected and unsullied by relationship with creatures. The Son does not exist eternally, but by an inscrutable divine decision to bring about creation—as if God were an isolated individual who then decides to come into relationship. Those who rejected Arius at Nicaea, in agreement with Athanasius, saw God as eternally giving, eternally relating. What we see in Jesus is what God eternally is. As Mike Higton puts it, God is love, all the way down.[26] So too David Jenkins loved to say that God is as he is in Jesus; therefore there is hope. Long ago, Williams argued that God's *intrinsic* life must be generative of relation: the creation makes full sense only in the light of a belief in the everlasting generation of the Son from the Father.[27]

Williams has consistently explored this position. Forty years later he writes that in the Incarnation, by God's initiative this divine Son is united with human nature. As we saw, human nature is always found only in particular agents. The particular agent here is Jesus. God is present not only with and in Jesus but *as* Jesus. Jesus is the finite and historical embodiment of the eternal Word. He is absolutely unique: fully divine and fully human. There are not two co-ordinated agencies at work in him, but "one Lord Jesus Christ". That is, there is a single moving principle, holding inseparably together action that is divine and action that is human. There is thus no way of understanding the human Jesus in abstraction from his union with the divine.[28]

The Incarnation is thus not the bare injection of divine qualities into a general human nature, abstracted from concrete human life. Quite the reverse. When the divine Sonship is embodied uninterruptedly as in the humanity of Jesus, the image of God in which humans were first created is fully activated.[29]

Moreover, as Mike Higton makes clear, if we are to share in the love between Father and Son, then it cannot be exhausted in that relationship, but must be open. There must be an "excess" in it, a capacity into which we can be drawn. This is the Holy Spirit, God's infinite capacity for new activity, especially for including new members in God's life. The Incarnation is the transcription into the historical world of the eternal relationship between Father and Son, the opening out of this relationship so that we can see it. And we do not just contemplate it at a distance. The power of the Spirit shapes us, drawing us into the Son's relationship with the Father; this is not something impersonal, but an active openness in the life of God, an active giving *of* the life of God, by God. We have to think of this active giving as a third "Person" in the eternal relational life which is God. And so we have God as Father, Son and Holy Spirit—as Trinity.[30] This thought was first worked out among the Cappadocian Fathers, Basil and the two Gregorys, and endorsed at the Council of Constantinople in 381. The Trinity is mystery—but we can dimly envisage the Persons enjoying an intensely intimate life quite beyond our imagination. The least inadequate word we have for this relationship is "Love". There is an eternal movement of giving and receiving in love between the Persons, a process of *kenosis* ("emptying").

So the Trinity is no remote abstraction, but is interwoven with the ordinary stuff of life. We need to avoid the idea of "God up there" and "us down here". Prayer, for example, is in the Spirit, with the Son, to the Father. We are caught up in a three-fold relational life—caught up by the Spirit into the Son's relationship with the Father. And, as Williams sees, the "we" extend through all human history; for it is the story of the discovery or realization of Jesus Christ in the faces of all people. The fullness of Christ is always *to be* discovered[31] (see the dedication of this book).

The Church

We have seen how the Son or Word is generated from the Father and lives in a filial relationship of obedience to the Father, and how this is rendered in narrative or dramatic terms in the earthly life of the Word incarnate. The eternal self-emptying (*kenotic*) exchange of love between Father and Son becomes active obedience by the Son even to the point of death (Philippians 2:8).

So the incarnate life of Christ is a revelation of the very nature of God. But at the same time, it is also a revelation of human nature, that its structure is really oriented towards realizing or expressing the Son's loving dependence on the Father. The eternal *Logos*, by realizing human possibility in a particular and unique way, creates a new set of relations between human and divine life. The finite and historical *kenosis* of the Son both realizes in history the eternal *kenosis* of the Word and opens the way for our finite and historical *kenosis* towards the Father. By incorporation into his body we can become aligned with his humanity.

It follows that if human beings live in communion with the Word incarnate, they are enabled to live in a way which reflects the life of the Trinitarian Persons in eternity, a life of mutual gift and self-emptying love. And just as the Trinitarian God lives eternally in a relationship with the created order that is free from conflict and competition, so the finite self, if united with the infinite reality of the Word, is also able to live in a reconciled communion with other human persons and to overcome the various life-denying divisions that bedevil the finite and fallen world.[32]

Rowan Williams draws again on the insights of St Maximus, who, as we saw, distinguished between a nature and an agent. A nature is an unchanging set of characteristics. In the case of humans, it does not exist apart from particular persons, who are agents making choices and pursuing goals. Because they are uniquely "in the image of God", humans are called to be active in a distinctively human way.

Maximus discusses the human predicament of sinfulness. He says that sin does not alter the definition of human nature: human nature remains the same through the drama of fall and redemption. What changes is the way in which it is active, and this can be altered by the relations in which an agent stands. Where our calling has been refused and overlaid with human sin, then what has to be restored is our capacity as finite human agents to choose and act as we should.

It is, however, not just a matter of restoration. When the *Logos* takes on human identity, it renders human nature capable of a new level of agency without its basic structure being changed. Humans are to be "filial", as the Word is filial, thankfully dependent on the self-gift of the Father, such that the fullness of that gift is lived in the life of the person who receives it. To be fully human is to be an adopted child of God, to receive the grace of becoming a daughter or son. In Maximus' terms, this is to partake of the operation of the divine nature, yet without ceasing to be created (cf. 2 Peter 1:4). We enter into this life at baptism.[33]

Moreover, this new level of agency is connected to the whole created order. For the relations thus created become the vehicle for a new level of transformative engagement with the cosmos. In personal union with the incarnate *Logos*, human agents are enabled to act as they are meant to act in regard to their entire human and non-human environment.[34]

In this whole process, Maximus sees not only *kenosis*, our self-emptying, but also *ekstasis*—"standing outside" ourselves, or our self-transcending in love. *Ekstasis* is the proper culmination of humanity's growth towards God. The knowing subject goes beyond its given limits, including the "natural" limits of self-preservation. *Ekstasis* is generated not by the self, but by *eros*, which Maximus uses without embarrassment for the magnetic drawing of finite beings towards the infinite. The believer is caught up into the self-abandoning love both of the Son for the Father and of God for creation. God has elected to live within the created order without ceasing to be what God eternally is. What God brings about in the finite is a movement of "desire", *eros*—a moving beyond what the intellect can master. This growth in love is also an overcoming of the divisions now prevailing in nature because of man's self-love: not only the divisions within the individual self, but within the community of finite agents. Human beings recognize more fully in one another their common nature as rational (*logikos*) and so become more and more solidly established in justice. So in contrast to the prevailing Western view of rationality as calculating utility, this universal rationality actually means the universal realization of "ecstasy", acting in other-directed love for all in their diverse conditions, so that believers belong not to themselves but to those whom they love.[35] This whole movement of thought in Maximus is thus profoundly integralist in its appreciation of the divine love.

We might well ask, "Who on earth would be opposed to such a vision being realized?" It is here that Rowan Williams confronts us with a recurring theme in his work. The Christian way, he warns, is irretrievably bound up with the themes of judgment and repentance—or, to put it less negatively, with conversion and transformation. The basic shape or narrative of being Christian is one of reversal and renewal. If the Paschal story is the bedrock of Christian identity, there is no escaping the pattern there of loss and recovery. Faith begins in a death: the literal death of Jesus for sedition and blasphemy, which is also the death of the bonds between him and his followers, and the "death" of whatever hope or faith had become possible in his presence prior to Good Friday; so that what becomes possible in his renewed presence at Easter has the character of a wholly creative, *ex nihilo* summons and enabling of hope and trust and action. All the strands of the Gospel tradition portray the dissolution of the apostolic band before the crucifixion and preserve the tradition of Peter's betrayal. The New Testament narrative presents us with *Christian* faith as that which the resurrection creates. Easter is inseparable from the cross of Christ. It is what is left after the judgment implied by the cross upon our human imagining. In the face of the cross, we see the lack of reality in our faith and hope, and we are left with no firm place to stand. "The 'shape' of Christian faith is the anchoring of our confidence beyond what we do or possess, in the reality of a God who freely gives to those needy enough to ask; a life lived 'away' from a centre in our own innate resourcefulness or meaningfulness", and so a life equipped to question and treat as provisional all our moral and spiritual achievement: it is "a life of *repentance in hope*."[36]

Nothing, says Williams, is more promising—and nothing is more difficult. The trouble is that the Church in every century of Christian history seeks to secure a faith that is not vulnerable to judgment, and to put cross and conversion behind it. But then it cuts itself off from the gift that lies beyond the void of the cross and imprisons itself in a self-understanding it can master and control. The question then is how the Church is to retain a faithful sense of the accessibility of God's promises. This particularly arises over dogma. For dogma has so often been understood as a sign of the Church's command of the data of revelation—a sign of something being settled rather than a challenge left open. But the possibilities of judgment and renewal must not be buried. The Church's dogmatic activity must always be conducted

> in order to give place to the freedom of God—the freedom of God from the Church's sense of itself and its power, and thus the freedom of God to renew and absolve. This is why dogmatic language becomes empty and even destructive of faith when it is isolated from a lively and converting worship and a spirituality that is not afraid of silence and powerlessness.

The more God is made to legitimize either ecclesiastical order or private religiosities, the easier it is to talk of God, and then the less such talk gives place to the freedom of God. There is a sense in which any dogmatic utterance should make it harder for us to talk about God.[37]

This also connects with Maximus, in that he too is concerned with finding the most appropriate vocabulary for talking of Christ, and also with the shape and sense of the baptized life, and more specifically the life of contemplation. Our understanding of Christ is inseparable from a theology of the Church and from holiness. Through the work of the Spirit in the Church and sacraments and contemplation, we can be delivered from a self-preoccupation that impedes both love and prayer. We are activated by a divine action that is eternally moving out towards the other. The finite order we inhabit is immeasurably diverse and of intricate complexity, and it is all destined to be drawn into harmony and mutual life-sharing through the reconciliation of humanity to God; and that reconciliation is already achieved in the self-emptying act of the Incarnation, which draws us into self-emptying and self-transcending faith and prayer; and so it naturally generates universal justice.[38]

Church, society and world

So the reality we live in is one of interwoven or interdependent, finite lives. And it is a reality which has been embraced by God and renewed and reconstituted in Christ. As Bonhoeffer puts it in his *Ethics*, in Jesus Christ the reality of God has entered into the reality of the world. It does not displace it but penetrates and suffuses it in such a way that we may participate in God's reality in and through participating in the world.[39]

For what God has done in Christ can only be declared and embodied in the community, and Christians are to be there with and for others: providing, working, struggling and suffering with and for them. The goal is to restore society and liberate it into the full range of human connectedness, in line with the unique connectedness established by God in Christ. For Christ is the centre of all human reality. And there is no part of the world, no matter how lost, which has not been accepted by God in Jesus Christ and reconciled to God. So all forms of basic human solidarity point to and are taken up into the fulfilled solidarity of the body of Christ; they are never in competition.[40]

Yet what is realized in Christ does not bring the immediate abolition of sin. This is true not only of society and the world, but also of Christians themselves. Thus if I am to be with and for others, that is constantly going to involve my death to self, a "No" to my own refusal of life and a "Yes" to continuing transformation. And that is true of the context in which I am set. The human *logos* is prone to see the divine *Logos* as the enemy, so far as it seeks to define itself as a solid thing over against divine life (in St Paul's language, to "live according to the flesh") and to see its entire social and material environment as existing only in relation to its own thoughts and needs. Indeed, every programme of human narration and sense-making is brought to silence here, and everything now depends on the underlying agency of God breaking through.[41]

It is easy here to slip into notions of two parallel realities, one sacred and the other profane or secular, and endless competition between them. It is therefore vital to grasp the eschatological character of the Christian faith. St Paul writes that if anyone is in Christ, that person is a new creation: "The old has passed away, behold the new has come. All this is from God, who through Christ reconciled us to himself and gave us the ministry of reconciliation." Yet he immediately goes on to say, "We beseech you on behalf of Christ, be reconciled to God" (2 Corinthians 5:17–20). On the one hand, God has taken decisive action in Christ for the salvation of the whole world. The believer is already by baptism translated into the new world, and so is the whole world in anticipation. But the powers of the old world are still vigorously at work, and Christ's work is incomplete. There is therefore a perpetual tension between what is realized and what is yet to come, culminating in God being all in all (cf. Romans 8; 1 Corinthians 15). We are living "between the times", between the "now" and the "not yet". The Church on earth, says Williams, is visible, but the space it occupies is not there to fight with the world for a piece of its territory or bring across as many of its inhabitants as possible. It is rather to bear witness to the world that it is still the world, that is, the world that is loved and reconciled by God. The Church is therefore engaged in an unceasing struggle for the whole world (and that of course includes itself) to become tangibly and historically what it actually already is.[42]

So the Church has to keep asking critical questions of society: whether any social action witnesses to and contributes to the most radical imaginable form of solidarity seen in Christ's humanity; for that is the solidarity of Creator and creation. Sometimes the existing social order will need to be disrupted because it is blocking the divine will. Bonhoeffer witnessed against the demand of the Nazi state for an oath of complete obedience. Certainly institutions and powers need to be called to account, if they accumulate vast profit, wealth and influence, or deny solidarity and a shared hunger for justice and peace.[43]

All this raises many questions about what mission and evangelization might mean in such a framework, and how the Church's worship might be conducted to bear witness to what God has done in Christ. In a world which insists on making sense of life on its own terms and promotes its own narrative, the Church could be a non-competitive and non-territorial sign of God's future. It could welcome the company of children, outcasts, and people with no status or claim. This would reflect Bonhoeffer's grounding of our responsibility for others in the wholly undefended humanity of Christ. For this shows most clearly the *difference* of God—the God who makes no competitive claim, but equally requires that we make no claim either, so that there is, in Bonhoeffer's words, an empty space in us into which God can move.[44]

Christ the heart of creation

At the end of Part 2, I raised the question of whether there might be a Creator "beyond" the universe, generative of it and within it from the very beginning. Part 3 and now Part 4 have presented an understanding of such a "Person"—indeed perhaps the only version which would fully respect the integrity of the finite.

Any embodiment of divine agency within the finite world must be in the form of genuine human action. In Christ, we see a coincidence of divine and human action, a life of divine initiative and prayerful dependence. The embodied reality of Jesus

> has the exact *effect* of divinity within the finite world: it "creates out of nothing", in the sense that it overcomes the consistent push towards dissolution and death in which humanity is trapped. It restores the divine image in creation and binds human persons into a holy community. It mends the breach between God and finite agents through the free bestowal of mercy and restoration of access to God in prayer.[45]

This finite agent Jesus acts in unbroken alignment with the way the Son/Word relates to God within the Trinity. So the Trinitarian life is the ground and type for bringing into being a finite world; the Word is the eternal form of dependence, and so is the ground and optimal form of all dependent, finite reality. So the relation between the Creator and creation is a complex where one cannot be spoken of without the other. The difference is that in the case of the Father and Son it is eternal and entirely reciprocal. In the case of creation, the relation is analogical: it has a beginning through God's free act; and it is asymmetrical: God would be God without the world, yet God has so acted as to be inconceivable outside this relation.[46]

So creation is most fully itself when it is aligned with God in dependency. It has a natural trajectory towards this kind of life-giving responsiveness. (This is entirely to accept evolution, and to recognize that there may be other instances in the universe.) Creation is at its optimal level of action and wellbeing when finite love and intelligence are in tune with the uncreated love and intelligence of the Word. It is in this sense that Jesus Christ is at the heart of creation. For us this is the restoration of a lost or occluded capacity in humanity—the capacity to be a mediating presence nurturing the harmony of the finite order in God, articulating its deepest meaning in terms of divine gift and divine beauty. So there can be a universal reconciliation, figured in the sacramental life of the body of Christ.[47]

God can do this only in and through a particular created agency that is capable of healing because it is entirely absorbed in the freedom of the infinite. So there is no gap to be bridged between infinite and finite. The human being is a mediating presence, a "middle" in creation, where meanings are drawn together, because it is the full animation of the material by the intelligent. But no finite being could do this. Ultimately God alone can be the "middle", bringing about the unity-in-multiplicity that is creation as a whole.[48]

This is the point where we hit up against our propensity to see God as an indefinitely magnified reflection of our ideas about power and freedom. It is actually as the unfree, the failing and suffering, that God realizes the focal and magnetic significance of the divine in the created world. For God to be the ground of the "rhythm" of finite reality, God must act in *and as* the unequivocally finite, whereas we are tempted to imagine divine liberty as exalted and insulated.[49]

Christ appears as the *perfectly creaturely*, animating the active, energetic interweaving of intelligible life that makes finite reality a *universe*, not a chaos. The finite is always related to the infinite cohesive agency of the Word, which gives it a *history* of responding to the gift of infinite love. For the supernatural is not something inserted into the natural, breaking its integrity. It is not an exalted version of the finite, or alongside the finite. Its difference is absolute—which is why it is possible for the infinite to be in and as the finite. It informs and permeates the finite, showing that there is no duality of God and the world, nor an identity of God and the world. If creation is a free and gratuitous bestowal of life, and not a necessity for God, then we must also hold to the integrity of the system of finite causes and interactions. And in such a world, God can only act from the centre of finite life, not as an intruder; otherwise the divine act simply dissolves the integrity of what is made.[50]

If this is the way the Trinitarian life is enacted on the plane of history, then our response must be our enactment of that life. We can never speak of God as an object. For God has invited us into God's own life. God's self-gift is made specific and historically real in the scandal of Christ's exclusion from the covenant community. This is no timeless proclamation. It is a genuinely transformative act, penetrating and pervading the whole of finite, vulnerable reality. The radical humiliation of Jesus demonstrates the divine repudiation of any project of becoming "like God" in Adam's way, trying to acquire powers unfairly withheld from humans by a self-protecting deity determined to defend his coercive authority. Our creaturely destiny is to be here on earth. The crucified Christ proclaims and makes possible "the patience of resting in the ordinary". This is not a form of passivity, but the way to release in finite reality the absolute self-dispossession of God's love.[51]

The specifically Christian affirmation is that the invisible God is made visible in the form of a man like any other (Philippians 2:7). Over against the drive of a sinful world to be "like God", the God who is "wholly God" appears as "wholly man", indeed, as a crucified slave.

> All that we do to protect ourselves against the consequences of our finitude—against our involvement with each other, the materiality of our lives and our indebtedness to our material environment, our mortality, our need to learn and change—is put radically in question by this divine embrace of the ordinary.

Only the Creator can exhibit fully what it is to be a creature and restore us to being creatures.[52]

Notes

1. Simon Jones (ed.), *The Sacramental Life: Gregory Dix and his Writings*, pp. ix–x.
2. Rowan Williams, *Christ the Heart of Creation*, pp. xi–xvi, his italics.
3. Mike Higton, *Difficult Gospel: The Theology of Rowan Williams*, pp. 1–5.
4. Rowan Williams, *On Christian Theology*, pp. 69–75.
5. Williams, *On Christian Theology*, p. 68.
6. Williams, *Christ the Heart of Creation*, p. 104.
7. Williams, *Christ the Heart of Creation*, pp. 102, 104.
8. Williams, *Christ the Heart of Creation*, p. 104.
9. Williams, *Christ the Heart of Creation*, pp. 100f., 104, 223.
10. On this last point see Williams, *On Christian Theology*, p. 77.
11. Williams, *On Christian Theology*, pp. 72, 76f.
12. Higton, *Difficult Gospel*, p. 20.
13. Williams, *On Christian Theology*, pp. 71f.
14. William Temple, *Personal Religion and the Life of Fellowship*, pp. 11f.
15. Williams, *Christ the Heart of Creation*, pp. 169f.
16. Williams, *Christ the Heart of Creation*, p. 183.
17. Higton, *Difficult Gospel*, pp. 21f.
18. Williams, *Christ the Heart of Creation*, p. 188.
19. Williams, *Christ the Heart of Creation*, pp. 185f.
20. Williams, *Christ the Heart of Creation*, p. 187.
21. Williams, *Christ the Heart of Creation*, pp. 188–90, his italics.
22. Williams, *Christ the Heart of Creation*, pp. 190f.
23. Williams, *Christ the Heart of Creation*, p. 191.
24. William Temple, *Readings in St John's Gospel*, p. 48.
25. Williams, *Christ the Heart of Creation*, p. 242.
26. Higton, *Difficult Gospel*, pp. 42f.
27. Rowan Williams, *The Wound of Knowledge*, p. 51 (second edition).
28. Williams, *Christ the Heart of Creation*, pp. 103, 109.
29. Williams, *Christ the Heart of Creation*, p. 108.
30. Higton, *Difficult Gospel*, pp. 56f.
31. Williams, *On Christian Theology*, pp. 172f.
32. Williams, *Christ the Heart of Creation*, pp. 106, 108, 221.
33. Williams, *Christ the Heart of Creation*, pp. 101–5.

[34] Williams, *Christ the Heart of Creation*, pp. 106f.
[35] Williams, *Christ the Heart of Creation*, pp. 107f.
[36] Williams, *On Christian Theology*, p. 83.
[37] Williams, *On Christian Theology*, pp. 83f.
[38] Williams, *Christ the Heart of Creation*, pp. 108f.
[39] Williams, *Christ the Heart of Creation*, p. 200.
[40] Williams, *Christ the Heart of Creation*, pp. 192, 201–6.
[41] Williams, *Christ the Heart of Creation*, pp. 192f.
[42] Williams, *Christ the Heart of Creation*, pp. 201f.
[43] Williams, *Christ the Heart of Creation*, pp. 203, 206, 213.
[44] Williams, *Christ the Heart of Creation*, pp. 213–15.
[45] Williams, *Christ the Heart of Creation*, pp. 219–21.
[46] Williams, *Christ the Heart of Creation*, pp. 221f.
[47] Williams, *Christ the Heart of Creation*, pp. 222f.
[48] Williams, *Christ the Heart of Creation*, pp. 223f.
[49] Williams, *Christ the Heart of Creation*, p. 225.
[50] Williams, *Christ the Heart of Creation*, pp. 226–8.
[51] Williams, *Christ the Heart of Creation*, pp. 234–7.
[52] Williams, *Christ the Heart of Creation*, pp. 237–9.

Epilogue

I began this work by making a fundamental critique of the state of our culture. I did this on a humanistic basic, which involved asking questions such as who we are as persons, what sort of a world we live in, what kinds of knowledge are open to us, and what is to count as rational. I then conducted a search for forms of the Christian faith which would underpin and root the position I had set out. This involved much clearing of the ground, particularly the questioning of the intense dualism which has in various forms been evident in the history of Western Christianity. I went on to propose the existence of a "Person" who would be both transcendent over the world process and immanent within it: not simply generative of it but intimately involved in the growth of the human spiral of knowing from the beginning. I briefly set out the integralist approach advocated by Henri de Lubac. I then showed forms of it in the writings of Gregory Dix on the Liturgy and Rowan Williams on the faith. In this way, I tried to exhibit a vision and stance of sufficient depth that it can address our cultural predicament for the sake of our common life together and provide a credible interweaving of worship, faith and action in the world. A fundamental critique was thus made through an interplay of fundamental philosophy and fundamental theology.

I make no apology for the level of thought involved. There is no good reason for thinking life is not complex, and Christianity does nothing to reduce the complexity. After all, it deals in ideas of finitude, which is to be related to the infinite, and of human frailty in relation to a God of love. And, as Rowan Williams pointed out, there is nothing simple in grasping the meaning for us of the statement "God is Love". Mike Higton was entirely right in giving his book on Williams' theology the title *Difficult Gospel*. It is vital to avoid treating these ideas as abstractions, and to connect them with concrete realities in the midst of our ordinary lives. One danger, as Bonhoeffer saw so well, is that Western Christians are prone to a false certainty that they know who Jesus is, and so fail to measure up to his radical challenge to us.

R. H. Tawney, in the middle of his book *Religion and the Rise of Capitalism*, declared that the social teaching of the Church had ceased to count because the Church itself had ceased to think. He was writing of the sixteenth century onwards, which saw the rise of impersonal finance, world markets and a capitalist organization of industry. Granted that we should love our neighbour as ourselves, the Church should have asked afresh under the new conditions who precisely is my neighbour, and how exactly I am to make my love effective in practice. It had, however, tried to moralize economic relations by treating every transaction simply as a case of individual conduct and responsibility, and endlessly repeated the duties of master to servant and servant to master. It had rightly insisted that all people were brothers and sisters. But it did not occur to it to point out that the brothers and sisters of the English merchant were the Africans kidnapped for slavery, the American Indians stripped of their lands, or the Indian craftsmen forced to sell their wares at starvation prices. This desiccated piety was no match for the intelligence and energy among the new breed of traders. It was not long before Christians comforted themselves with the notion that for the transactions of economic life, no moral principles exist.[1] Tawney's observations have an urgent relevance to today's world and demand that the Church think in depth. Each Christian has a unique calling, but none should deny the importance of the Church engaging strenuously with the modern world, or dismiss those who think deeply on their behalf.

Christianity is a complete way of life. Christians therefore have continually to examine what is happening in their culture and simultaneously immerse themselves in their faith in order to live out the gospel. They have the privilege of working out the right attitudes and thoughts and the best courses of action as they experience life in an ever-shifting world. As I re-read that section of Tawney, I realize that William Temple did take him to heart and become far more incisive in his last ten years.

The volume of essays *Anglican Social Theology* gives a spectrum of strands across the English Anglican tradition, as well as visiting the interface between Roman Catholicism and Anglicanism with Anna

Rowlands. I warmly commend her recent book, *Towards a Politics of Communion: Catholic Social Teaching in Dark Times*, which, in contrast to the perceived naïve optimism of that tradition, reveals its sheer weight and depth as it grapples with the brokenness of the contemporary world. For those who count themselves English Evangelicals, Jonathan Chaplin's chapter on "Evangelical Contributions to the Future of Anglican Social Theology" is striking in its assessment of the state of English Evangelicalism. All the chapters give leads for further reading. Rowan Williams himself has continually been exploring the interface between faith and life, and among his published books I particularly commend his collection *Faith in the Public Square*. There is also an extensive digital archive of his time as Archbishop of Canterbury.

We need continually to rethink, through our experience of living, the relationship between the hoary Anglican trio of scripture, tradition and reason. William Temple used to say that revelation is not a set of truths to be formulated in propositions but is personal communication given in events. The supreme criterion for the Christian life is the revelation of God in Jesus Christ, of which scripture is the inspired written record. Thus the primary *Logos* of God is the living Person Jesus Christ. Tradition also is vital; for one could not come to faith except through the tradition embodied in the Church. Yet there is no safety in simply handing it down. Tradition is also the experience of Christians living adventurously in response to those central revelatory events. And since they inhabit societies and cultures which grow and change, they must take account of new knowledge, which will involve the critical and constructive use of reason, in a continuing dialogue with all seeking to understand and shape life in its diverse facets. On the issue of finance, world markets and capitalism, we should by now be at least as good as the Victorian novelist Elizabeth Gaskell in *Mary Barton* and *North and South*. We should listen again to the numerous pithy and pungent observations of Tawney, for example, that though no individual by taking thought can add one cubit to their stature, a nation by doing so can add an inch to the height of children and a pound to their weight; and that this requires public, collective action, which is no more than the fulfilment of the injunction, "Bear one another's burdens".[2]

"The Christian religion is primarily a religion of redemption, a gospel. It is good news, not a philosophy or good advice." Those are the words of the distinguished Anglican theologian Vigo A. Demant. He goes on, "The good news is that God, who is the source and end of the created order, is by an act of divine initiative restoring things to their true nature. In Jesus Christ, God the Son, the creative power of God... purifies and transforms the actual creation." Demant was writing in 1939, immediately before the Second World War. That context revealed starkly "the facts of human nature", as he put it, "the contradiction in [humanity]". Its restoration cannot be effected or sustained by self-improvement, only by an act of God. Humans need to recognize their real centre in God, and acknowledge the sin which makes them deviate from that centre. This is true of all people, and that includes Christians themselves. The trouble is that they become trapped in unstable philosophies pressing upon them in their environment, and obsessed with morality: what I supposedly ought to be doing.[3] So this book has avoided giving advice; it has focussed on exposing skewed and false philosophies and ideologies, and on discerning the foundations of culture and the Christian life.

The primary task of Christians is to be centred on God and not on self, and to recognize their entire dependence on God. Our fidelity to God depends on God's fidelity to us. William Temple wrote in *Readings in St John's Gospel*: "It is the service of God which we must above all be ready to accept... Our first thought must never be, 'What can I do for God?' The answer to that is, Nothing. The first thought must always be, 'What can God do for me?'"[4]

Notes

[1] R. H. Tawney, *Religion and the Rise of Capitalism: A Historical Study*, pp. 187–9.
[2] R. H. Tawney, *Equality*, p. 139.
[3] Vigo A. Demant, *The Religious Prospect*, pp. 232–4.
[4] William Temple, *Readings in St John's Gospel*, p. 210.

Appendix 1: Exclusion and Embrace

The two stories in our Gospel reading for today—the Lost Sheep and the Lost Coin (Luke 15:1–10) are very familiar; and perhaps even more so is the parable of the Prodigal Son (15:11–32). So it is easy to think we know *the* meaning. But as with any rattling good story, there's more than one meaning, and there are always new meanings to be discovered. I found a reading of the parable of the Prodigal Son that was new to me. It was in a book called *Exclusion and Embrace*. I am going to share that reading with you now.

The story begins, "There was a man who had two sons." So let's read it just as a story: let's stay with the characters—who they are, and how they relate to one another—and see the twists and turns as the story unfolds.

"Honour your father and mother." That was bedrock for the Israelites. The younger son breaks that commandment by brazenly going to his father and demanding, "Father, give me the share of property that falls to me." It is like saying, "I'm sick of waiting for you to drop dead." His ploy succeeds, and soon he is off, taking everything with him. So the son terminates his relation with his father.

He squanders his inheritance, and as he has severed his ties with home, he has to hitch himself to a foreigner, and degrade himself by looking after pigs. It's a kind of exodus in reverse: the Jewish family bond has been exchanged for an Egyptian bondage. So when he "comes to himself", it is not a self he is exactly happy with. He says, "How many of my father's hired servants . . . " That is more like envy than repentance. But the words are very revealing. For there, buried within him, is the *memory* of being a son. "Coming to himself" cannot be separated from knowing that he belongs: he always was his father's son, and he still is.

But of course he is no longer a son pure and simple. For he has betrayed the relationship. He declares himself a "son-no-longer-worthy-to-be-called-a-son". So he constructs his speech to his father. He will confess his fault, and hope for acceptance as a hired servant.

Let us now turn to the father. The father has coped with his younger son's rudeness, divided the property, and let him go. But he does not let him go out of their relationship. His eyes search for him continually, and finally catch sight of him in the distance. Though away in a far country, the son has remained in the father's prayerful heart. And what does he do?

In compassion he *runs*—he doesn't make a risk assessment or care about his dignity—he runs, and he embraces him and kisses him. He accepts him back as the son he still is. And his initiative turns the son's strategy on its head. First comes the acceptance—only then the confession. And yes, there does need to be a confession. But even that confession is cut short, and the son is decked out as an honoured son. Notice the language the father uses. It is not the language of worthy/unworthy. No, he says, "For this my son was dead and is alive again, he was lost and is found." What is going on here? For that we have to turn to the older brother.

The older brother hears the music and dancing and learns that his younger brother is back. He is angry and refuses to go in, so his father has to come out to plead with him. Back come the words, "this son of yours . . . " He has clearly excluded his brother from his heart long ago, and will not make space for him now. Moreover, he does not respectfully address his father as "Father". So even as the father welcomes back the one son, he faces double trouble: a hard division between the brothers *and* a rupture in his relation with his other son. Why is the older son so bitter?

It is because the father has broken some basic rules—rules that are vital for any true family or social life. In Deuteronomy 21:18–21, if a man is stubborn, rebellious and disobedient to his father or mother, then he is to be brought before the elders of the city, and all the men of the city are to stone him to death. It's there in black and white. Besides, the older brother can complain that *he* has behaved better but fared worse. He has worked away for years for less recognition than the brother who squandered the inheritance. Put simply, if there is no justice, there will be no home. The household will fall apart, and we'll all be in a distant country starving. Surely it all makes perfect sense. If you mess up, you pay the just penalty.

I think the story offers a subtle response to that logic. First it suggests that if we fixate on rules, we are in danger of distorting the truth of the situation. The older brother portrays himself as having been like an obedient slave of his father. And he blackens his brother by claiming that he has blown the father's money on women. His approach leads to self-righteousness, polarization and the demonizing of another. So what is the heart of the matter? Is it rules, and we just need to apply them flexibly? Or is there something more profound? For the answer to that we need to return to the father.

It certainly looks at first sight as if the father is a sentimental old fool, pitifully wrecking family relations through his moral weakness. But the father does not say, "Oh, forget it!" The son's betrayal has deeply wounded the father, and confession was necessary before there could be a celebration. But he doesn't let rules have the last word. And though the older brother in his moral rage is also rude to his father, again he doesn't let rules have the last word. The father appeals to something above and beyond moralizing. It was necessary, he says, to rejoice and be glad. Yes, there is a "must" over salutary rules; but there is also a "must" in receiving back one who has broken the rules. He is determined that both sons shall truly be sons to him, and brothers to one another.

So relationships have priority over all rules. The older brother employs moral ideas of bad/good. The father knows how important these are, but he refuses to allow moral rules to have the final say. Instead he employs relational ideas of lost/found, and dead/alive. Relationships are prior to moral performance, and they are not based in moral performance. As the story twists this way and that, he has to continually keep adjusting, creatively rebuilding broken identities and relationships. The quest for reconciliation and unity is a very difficult journey, but he doesn't get lost in it, because fundamentally he is guided, not by rules or laws, but by unwavering love. And in this way he does maintain the family order—not by exclusion, but by embrace.

Does that interpretation make sense? I think we can first ask that of our ordinary human experience of living in families or social groups. Jenny and I knew that for our marriage to flourish we needed constantly to keep adjusting our relationship to one another, and to keep open the lines of communication with our children. For many years, I worked for an organization combatting child sexual exploitation. At one conference, an anguished mother came forward to tell how she had lost her daughter to a man who had mercilessly groomed her. She complained that social services, to whom she'd repeatedly turned, in the end told her that her child had made her life-choice and she should let her go. She couldn't, and I am sure she was right. Behind the attitude of the social services was not so much rigid moral rules, but the modern Western notion that we are really individual atoms who have to claim our freedom and autonomy, and any relationships worth having are entirely self-chosen. The mother knew otherwise and kept the daughter in her heart.

And what of a Christian perspective? Well, first you need to see the story in the context of Jesus' ministry. We are not told how the older brother responds. And it is not hard to see why. At the beginning of Luke 15, we are told that the Pharisees and the scribes murmur, saying, "This man receives sinners and eats with them." The parable puts an immense challenge to them. Jesus is saying to them in effect, "You are acting like the older brother. You believe that we must strictly observe every bit of the law for God's Kingdom to come. And so, when I claim the Kingdom is already here in my words and deeds, in my whole person, you think I am leading Israel astray, so that the Kingdom will never come." It comes down to a sharp and stark choice. Either Jesus is truly God's Son, or he is a mortal threat to the people of Israel, and to the delicate balance of relations with Rome. For Caiaphas, it became expedient that one man should die for the people. And so he did—in a way far more profound than Caiaphas ever knew.

And let's put that in the wider context of the great story we are here today to celebrate. What are the deepest truths within the Old and New Testaments which are also embedded in the Eucharistic Prayer we shall presently hear? God created the world entirely out of love, and is ever with it and for it, enabling it to flourish. Within that world God creates a particular people, giving them a covenant: "I will take you for my people, and I will be your God" (Exodus 6:7). When they are perverse and unfaithful, God remains faithful to his promises. The prophets, especially Hosea, forcefully expose the unfaithfulness of Israel and look to the faithfulness of God. Even when the Israelites are sent off into exile, God brings the lost and strayed back.

That story reaches its climax in the life, death and resurrection of Jesus Christ. Here we see the perfect demonstration of what God is like. He goes after the lost, recklessly leaving the ninety-nine exposed in the wilderness. At the Last Supper, God in Christ renews the covenant, making his disciples honoured guests, even ahead of their ultimate betrayal. He refounds Israel, and, when death cannot hold him and he is raised, the Holy Spirit is given to animate the members of Christ's body, the Church. What happened in his life can happen in theirs. And it is now a belonging which is open absolutely to all—way beyond the confines of Israel. God still seeks with great earnestness the lost and the strayed, wherever they are, including us:

> Perverse and foolish oft I stray'd,
> But yet in love He sought me,
> And on His shoulder gently laid,
> And home, rejoicing, brought me. (H. W. Baker)

The Kingdom is already here and active—but its completion, when God will be all in all, is not yet—but it is assured.

I would like to suggest that the Western Church, Catholic and Protestant, has all too often focussed on obeying the rules. A priest once said to me that Christians were particularly prone to suffer from the disease known as the "hardening of the oughteries". Well, rules have their rightful place. But that easily becomes either a way of playing safe, or a harsh morality. Pope Francis has encouraged people to focus on relationships and to take generous risks. I was glad to quote from his letter on *The Joy of Love* at Heather and John's wedding reception a year ago. But above all we need to take our cue from God as revealed in Christ, and from this parable. We should focus firmly on God's energetic and unwavering love, shown to the full on the Cross, and we should ourselves live lives which are creative, adventurous and imaginative, aiming constantly to widen the circle of belonging, here and now in our ordinary, day-to-day lives.

And that, it seems to me, is what our Breathing Space project here is about. It is there to enhance the quality of our living, drawing people together by a range of activities, like Men's Shed, mindfulness, creative writing and Woodland Wonders, offering people of all ages the chance to appreciate the world we live in, and, it is to be hoped, widening that circle of belonging. Because that is in line with God's unwavering love for us all.

Finally, who, you may ask, wrote the book *Exclusion and Embrace*? A man called Miroslav Volf. He is of mixed parentage, but is a Croatian citizen who, when Yugoslavia disintegrated and Croatia claimed independence, witnessed Serbian forces invade, herd his people into concentration camps, rape women, burn down churches and destroy cities. He wanted to take very seriously Christ's call for us to embrace our enemies as God in Christ has embraced us. But could he embrace a Serbian fighter? More broadly, he is deeply disturbed by the way so many people now are hated simply for their otherness. Exclusion, he believes, skews our perceptions of reality, so that we react out of fear and anger to all those who are not within our ever-narrowing circle. Salvation, he believes, is not only this-and-that individual being reconciled to God; it also means learning to live with one another—and that may well call for the dangerous and costly step of opening ourselves to the other, and enfolding him or her in the same embrace with which God enfolds us. I do not have a God's-eye view of Brexit, but I would point to the distortion, polarization and demonizing, often shot through with self-righteousness. And the Referendum of 2016 did not create but exposed the latent divisions in our own nation, over how we read our story, who we now are, our relationships with others, and where we go from here. Christ surely challenges us, too, to learn how to walk the road of reconciliation and unity!

Address given on 15 September 2019

Miroslav Volf, *Exclusion and Embrace: A Theological Exploration of Identity, Otherness and Reconciliation*, esp. pp. 156–65.

Appendix 2: "What more do you want from me?"

So here we are at the first Sunday in Lent. What are we to do about it? Are we going to give something up for Lent? Or are we going to do something extra? Or a bit of both? Do by all means attend the sessions on Pilgrimage. The basic question is, What can we do which will mean that by the end of Lent we are living closer to our Lord?

William Temple's *Readings in St John's Gospel* were the fruit of thirty years of reflection. When he comments on Christ's washing of the disciples' feet at the Last Supper, he remarks that this is Christ's way of displaying Divine Majesty. Temple writes: "We rather shrink from this revelation. We are ready perhaps to be humble before God; but we do not want him to be humble in his dealings with us.... [But] the divine humility shews itself in rendering service. He who is entitled to claim the service of all his creatures chooses first to give his service to them. *Our* humility does not begin with the giving of service; it begins with the readiness to receive it. Our first thought must never be, 'What can I do for God?' The answer to that is, Nothing. The first thought must always be, 'What would God do for me?'" (pp. 209f.).

That thought lies deep in the tradition, and of course is rooted in Christ's words: "The Son of man came not to be served but to serve, and to give his life as a ransom for many" (Mark 10:45). Some years ago a member of the Eastern Orthodox Church gave me this wax tablet with words from St John Chrysostom—St John "golden mouth", for he was a very eloquent speaker. It is headed "What more do you want from me?" "I will serve you, for I have come to minister, not to be ministered unto.... I have become poor and a wanderer for your sake, I died on the cross and was buried for your sake; I rose to heaven to entreat my Father on your behalf... You are everything to me: co-heir, brother and sister, friend, a member of my body. Why do you turn away from him who loves you? Why do you toil for temporal things? What more do you want from me?"

So perhaps these words give a clue to what we might do this Lent. Put another way, we can take up the strapline of Breathing Space: we can pause, ponder, reflect and slow down. For we surely live in a frenetic world. We belong to the generation who are for ever on the go, multi-tasking, doing everything in the least possible time. But there are many things which require a lot of time if they are to be learned and done well—and living the Christian life involves lifelong learning. So let us look at the readings for today.

Let's have a good look at the first reading, the passage from Deuteronomy (26:1-11). Deuteronomy is the last of the five books of the law. At its root the word for "law" in Hebrew means "direction" or "guidance"—God gives the Israelites the guidance they need for living as a community. Here we discover the very roots of that community. When they settle in the land they are to *remember*. And when I say remember, I do not mean a bare mental recall of some fact like a date in history. It is something they are to live by, because it gives basic meaning to their lives. And that recalling involves doing something—a performance. They take the first of all the fruit of the ground and put it in a basket, and they take it to the priest, who sets it down before the altar of the Lord. And every Israelite is to say, "I declare this day to the Lord your God that I have come into the land which the Lord swore to our fathers to give us."

This is the language of belonging. Every Israelite belongs to the community—so much so that they all speak as if they have just come into the land—they are one with their ancestors who first occupied the land. And they are one also with those who lived before that—those who went down into Egypt and became slaves of the Egyptians. They had then become so demoralized they had ceased to be a people, and become more like a rabble. But God had heard their cry for help and had brought them out of slavery, and made them a people by guiding them through the wilderness and giving them the law and then the land—a land flowing with milk and honey. This is their common story or narrative, and they are to live by it—inhabit the land, and inhabit the story. And that story extended even further back—for they believed that God had made a promise to their wandering fathers, Abraham, Isaac and Jacob, to give the land to their descendants.

So the people are to rejoice in all the good which the Lord their God has given to them—to each of them and to their house. The word "give" occurs six times in eleven verses. The giving clearly flows from a God who is, yes, mysterious and eternal—but is clearly to be thought of in at least personal terms—God is one whose very nature is to give and give and give. God is one who makes promises and can be relied on to keep them. God can be entirely trusted to remember—there's that word again: God remembers his promises by doing what he has promised to do. Put very simply, God is always with them and for them. The passage speaks of God's name dwelling with them. It is an odd phrase. "Name" means God is truly there—but it also warns the Israelites not to commit the folly of taking God for granted and using of God for their own ends. They must remember what God has done in their service and respond by worshipping God and following the guidance God has given them. Actually, much of the Old Testament turns out to be the story of how the Israelites perversely and obstinately fail to be faithful in response. Well, at least they preserved in their scriptures the story of what God has done for them—and the story of their own perversity!

And so Psalm 91 gives us a portrait of the person who takes God for refuge and fortress and shows perfect trust. When that person calls on God, God will answer and be with them. They will enjoy a long life and be shown God's salvation.

The passage from Romans (10:8b–13) shows us the transition from the old to the new. God's faithfulness to those promises has now been revealed to the full through Jesus Christ: God has vindicated him, by raising him from the dead, so that Jesus himself is Lord, the one on whom salvation depends. And there is no distinction now between Jew and Greek, that is, gentile. The same Lord is Lord of all, and gives his riches to all who call upon him: everyone who calls upon the name of the Lord will be saved. At the end of the Deuteronomy passage, even the "sojourner" or resident alien among the Israelites is also called upon to rejoice. Now the call and invitation has been extended to every single person on the planet. And so it is that we are here today, graciously incorporated into Christ's body and inheritors of all the promises of God. Through him we have a solidarity not only with those around us but with everyone on the planet. If one suffers, we all suffer.

And so we come to the passage from Luke (4:1-13)—the temptations of Christ. Jesus has just been baptized, accepting his unique calling from God to live out his life in total faithfulness to God: to show just what God is like—*and* to show what human life should be like. Even we can appreciate that such a call was bound to be fraught for Jesus, given that he was stepping into public life in a country occupied by the Romans and awash with expectations that a Messiah would come from God to eject them, so that the Jews would be able once again to occupy the land under the reign of God in prosperity and peace. What sort of a Messiah was he to be? That is surely the question running through the temptations. If God is a God of infinite power, then why not a Messiah who solves their basic material needs: makes the land flow again with milk and honey? Why not drive out the Romans by force and replace them with a native Jewish kingdom under God, presumably bristling with military hardware against all comers? Or why not prove to all your status as Messiah by performing superhuman feats of power? To which the reply is, "You shall not tempt the Lord your God." You cannot bolster your power with divine power: that would be to use God for your own ends—for your own glory. No, that is completely to misunderstand God. And notice even the devil quotes scripture—the very Psalm 91 that we sang earlier. So you cannot assume that you can simply pick up the Bible and read out of it whatever you want. Scripture is to be understood by living in a community and working out together how it is to be understood and lived out in the circumstances we face. And that is surely far from easy. So our best chance of getting it right is to learn to trust in God: to worship, to read the scriptures, to pray, to pause, ponder, reflect a little and slow down: to wait on God, which is what Lent, like Advent, is about.

If we look ahead to Jesus' ministry, we see a man who upholds the complete trustworthiness of God. He calls people to discipleship with a message of loving acceptance by God. He does not seek or defend any space for himself but gives himself without limit for the sake of others. He pushes aside old rituals and all kinds of social boundaries, to call women and men his sisters and brothers and friends. He draws the marginalized back into full membership, literally touching those who are rejected as unclean and eating with all and sundry. He attacks the Jewish leaders whose regulations set up barriers against access to God. For undermining these divisions and exclusions he quickly encounters opposition from the Jewish authorities. They seek every way of discrediting him and persuade themselves that he is an imposter. There had to be a showdown, and that was bound to take place in Jerusalem. Luke tells us later (9:51, when we are less than halfway through the Gospel) that Jesus set his face to go up to Jerusalem.

At the end of the temptations, we are told that the devil departed from Jesus "until an opportune time". That time came when Jesus was finally arrested in the Garden of Gethsemane, where Luke tells us that Jesus says, "This is your hour, and the power of darkness" (22:53). He has prayed that the disciples may not enter into temptation, and then for himself, "Father, if thou art willing, remove this cup from me; nevertheless not my will, but thine, be done" (22:42). An angel appears to strengthen him. And we are told he was in agony and sweat poured off him. What we see in the hours which follow is the full revelation of what kind of a Messiah we are given. His whole ministry has been a self-emptying—a humble and vulnerable life, in solidarity with all and especially the weak and poor, one continuous appeal of free, unconditional love. That is the way he judges us—not by zapping us, but by appealing to us. To the end that is the love that is freely given, even when he is totally unfree, immobile. He is crucified between two thieves, one of whom recognizes him, the other doesn't. So the question is put to us: can we accept *this* kind of Messiah, one who will not coerce my response, but appeals to us by love alone? Can we believe that in Christ we see not only what it is to be human—but also who God is. If, as Paul tells us in 2 Corinthians, God was in Christ, reconciling the world to himself, then the God with whom we have to do is a God of pure and infinite love, and we can allow ourselves to be drawn by his trust and commitment to us, and so gladly express our trust in him in response.

That response needs to come from each and every one of us. But it is not just an individual matter. Jesus' task in his ministry was not just to call individuals but to reshape and re-form the people of Israel into a new community. We are called to be the body of Christ, to live out of his life as a community here in Witton Gilbert, sharing in people's anguish and joy, living in solidarity with them. And so we gather here each week to enter into that life more fully, as individuals and as a community, and we then disperse to live it out in the particular circumstances in which we live. And here we have Breathing Space, our main mission arm, to give corporate expression to our response to the life-giving gift of Jesus Christ to us and to the world. It is Christ working in us to help people to find life, and find it in all its abundance.

But first we need to set aside time to receive—to let Christ serve us. We are to pause, ponder, reflect and slow down. And perhaps it is better if I end this address not with words but with music, especially at this time of tragedy and violence. I cannot think of anything better than a beautiful piece by Franz Liszt. Liszt knew Alphonse de Lamartine, who was a French MP for many years. He actually declared the Second French Republic in 1848 from a balcony in Paris. Very surprisingly he also wrote religious poetry, including *Poetic and religious harmonies*. Liszt responded to the poems by writing a set of pieces for the piano, with the same title. I will play you the first part of the piece called "The Blessing of God in Solitude". Lamartine writes, "Whence comes, my God, this peace which floods me?" It fuses divine love and human love, and expresses a deep gratitude to God for the gift of life.

May the peace of Christ, crucified and risen, flood our hearts too. Amen.

Address given on the first Sunday of Lent, 6 March 2022

Franz Liszt, *Harmonies poétiques et religieuses*. "Bénédiction de Dieu dans la solitude", is also published by G. Henle Verlag as a single edition, and Lamartine's poem of the same title prefixes the score. Another piece is "Funérailles", which salutes the fallen of the Hungarian Revolution of 1848, ruthlessly crushed by Austria, but can equally address us and move us over contemporary tragedy and brutality.

Liszt, *Harmonies poétiques et religieuses*, Saskia Giorgini (piano), with very illuminating notes by her and Mark Berry. Pentatone PTC 5186 296.

Bibliography

Anglican–Roman Catholic International Commission, *The Final Report* (London: SPCK, 1981).
Ayer, A. J., *Language, Truth and Logic* (London: Gollancz, 1946; first published 1936).
Bailey, Simon, *A Tactful God: Gregory Dix, Priest, Monk and Scholar* (Leominster: Gracewing, 1995).
Balthasar, Hans Urs von, *The Theology of Henri de Lubac: An Overview*, A Communio Book (San Francisco: Ignatius Press, 1991).
Barenboim, Daniel, *Everything is Connected: The Power of Music* (London: Weidenfeld and Nicolson, 2008).
Barenboim, Daniel and Said, Edward W., *Parallels and Paradoxes: Explorations in Music and Society*, edited and with a preface by Ara Guzelimian (London: Bloomsbury, 2003).
Book of Common Prayer, The (Society for Promoting Christian Knowledge, no date).
Bowra, C. M., *The Greek Experience* (London: Weidenfeld and Nicolson, 1957).
Bradshaw, Paul F. and Johnson, Maxwell E., *The Eucharistic Liturgies: Their Evolution and Interpretation* (London: SPCK, 2012).
Brevint, Daniel, *The Christian Sacrament and Sacrifice* (Delhi: Sagwan Press, 2018).
Brown, Malcolm (ed.), *Anglican Social Theology: Renewing the Vision Today* (London: Church House Publishing, 2014).
Brown, Malcolm, "The Case for Anglican Social Theology Today" and "Anglican Social Theology Tomorrow", in Brown, Malcolm (ed.), *Anglican Social Theology: Renewing the Vision Today* (London: Church House Publishing, 2014), pp. 1–27 and 175–89.

Bunting, Madeleine, *Love of Country: A Hebridean Journey* (London: Granta Books, 2016).
Carney, Mark, *Value(s): Building a Better World for All* (London: William Collins, 2021).
Chaplin, Jonathan, "Evangelical Contributions to the Future of Anglican Social Theology", in Brown, Malcolm (ed.), *Anglican Social Theology: Renewing the Vision Today* (London: Church House Publishing, 2014), pp. 102–32.
Common Worship: Services and Prayers for the Church of England (London: Church House Publishing, 2000).
Crockett, William R., "Holy Communion", in Sykes, Stephen and Booty, John (eds), *The Study of Anglicanism* (London and Minneapolis: SPCK/Fortress Press, 1988), pp. 272–85.
Crockett, William R., *Eucharist: Symbol of Transformation* (Collegeville, MN: Liturgical Press, 1989).
Demant, Vigo A., *The Religious Prospect* (London: Muller, 1939, 1941).
Descartes, René, *Discourse on Method and The Meditations*, Translated with an Introduction by F. E. Sutcliffe (London: Penguin Books, 1968).
Dix, Gregory, *The Shape of the Liturgy* (London: Dacre Press, Adam and Charles Black, 1945).
Duffy, Eamon, *The Stripping of the Altars: Traditional Religion in England, 1400–1580* (Yale University Press, 2005).
Francis, Pope, *The Joy of Love (Amoris Laetitia): On Love in the Family* (Gilbert, AZ: Wellspring, 2016).
Frankopan, Peter, *The Silk Roads: A New History of the World* (London: Bloomsbury, 2015).
Friedman, Milton, *Capitalism and Freedom* (Chicago: University of Chicago Press, 1962).
Graham, Elaine, *Between a Rock and a Hard Place: Public Theology in a Post-Secular Age* (London: SCM Press, 2013).
Hayek, Friedrich A., *The Road to Serfdom* (London: Routledge & Kegan Paul, 1944/1962).
Hayek, Friedrich A., *Law, Legislation and Liberty, Vol. 2: The Mirage of Social Justice* (London: Routledge & Kegan Paul, 1976).

Hebert, A. G., *Liturgy and Society: The Function of the Church in the Modern World* (London: Faber and Faber, 1935).

Hebert, A. G. (ed.), *Parish Communion: A Book of Essays* (London: SPCK, 1939).

Higgins, Charlotte, "Taking down statues is not 'censorship'", *The Guardian*, 21 January 2021.

Higton, Mike, *Difficult Gospel: The Theology of Rowan Williams* (London: SCM Press, 2004).

Hughes, John, "After Temple? The Recent Renewal of Anglican Social Thought", in Brown, Malcolm (ed.), *Anglican Social Theology: Renewing the Vision Today* (London: Church House Publishing, 2014), pp. 74–101.

Iremonger, F. A., *William Temple, Archbishop of Canterbury: His Life and Letters* (London: Oxford University Press, 1948).

Ivison, Irene, *Fiona's Story: A Tragedy of our Times* (London: Virago, 1997).

Jenkins, David E., *The Glory of Man* (London: SCM Press, 1967).

Jones, Simon (ed.), *The Sacramental Life: Gregory Dix and His Writings* (Norwich: Canterbury Press, 2007).

Kleeman, Jenny, *Sex Robots and Vegan Meat: Adventures at the Frontier of Birth, Food, Sex & Death* (London: Picador, 2020).

Klein, Naomi, *On Fire: The Burning Case for a Green New Deal* (London: Allen Lane, 2019).

Kuhn, Thomas, *The Structure of Scientific Revolutions* (Chicago: University of Chicago Press, 1962).

Lent, Jeremy, *The Patterning Instinct: A Cultural History of Humanity's Search for Meaning* (Amherst NY: Prometheus Books, 2017).

Liszt, Franz, *Harmonies poétiques et religieuses*, including "Bénédiction de Dieu dans la solitude" and "Funérailles" (München: G. Henle Verlag, 2010).

Liszt, Franz, *Harmonies poétiques et religieuses*, Saskia Giorgini (piano). (Pentatone Music, 2021, PTC 5186 296).

MacIntyre, Alasdair, *After Virtue: A Study in Moral Theory* (London: Duckworth, 1981, second edition 1985).

MacIntyre, Alasdair, *Whose Justice? Which Rationality?* (London: Duckworth, 1988).

MacIntyre, Alasdair, *Three Rival Versions of Moral Enquiry: Encyclopaedia, Genealogy, and Tradition* (London: Duckworth, 1990).
Mason, Rowena, Harding, Luke and Davies, Harry, "The Tory Donor King", *The Guardian*, 6 October 2021, p. 11.
Milbank, John, *The Suspended Middle: Henri de Lubac and the Renewed Split in Modern Catholic Theology* (Grand Rapids, MI / Cambridge: Wm B. Eerdmans, 2014).
Olusoga, David, *Black and British: A Forgotten History* (London: Pan Books, 2016).
O'Toole, Fintan, *Heroic Failure: Brexit and the Politics of Pain* (London: An Apollo Book, Head of Zeus, 2018).
Pasternak, Boris, *Doctor Zhivago*, translated from the Russian by Max Hayward and Manya Harari (London: Collins, 1958; Collins Fontana Books, 1961; original Russian published in Milano: Feltrinelli Editore, 1958).
Peacocke, Arthur R., *Creation and the World of Science* (Oxford: Clarendon Press, 1979).
Peacocke, Arthur R., *Paths from Science towards God: The End of all our Exploring* (Oxford: Oneworld Publications, 2001).
Piketty, Thomas, *Capital and Ideology* (Cambridge, MA and London: The Belknap Press of Harvard University Press, 2020).
Pius XII, Pope, *Humani Generis* (London: Catholic Truth Society, 1950, 1959).
Plato, *The Republic*, Translated with an Introduction by H. D. P. Lee (Harmondsworth: Penguin Books, 1955).
Plato, *The Last Days of Socrates* (including *Phaedo*), Translated and with an Introduction by Hugh Tredennick (Harmondsworth: Penguin Books, 1954, 1959, 1969).
Polanyi, Michael, *Personal Knowledge: Towards a Post-Critical Philosophy* (London: Routledge & Kegan Paul, 1958).
Rogers, Nicholas, *Murder on the Middle Passage: The Trial of Captain Kimber* (Woodbridge: The Boydell Press, 2020).

Rowlands, Anna, "Fraternal Traditions: Anglican Social Theology and Catholic Social Teaching in a British Context", in Brown, Malcolm (ed.), *Anglican Social Theology: Renewing the Vision Today* (London: Church House Publishing, 2014), pp. 133–74.

Rowlands, Anna, *Towards a Politics of Communion: Catholic Social Teaching in Dark Times* (London: T&T Clark Bloomsbury Publishing, 2021).

Sandel, Michael J., *Justice: What's the Right Thing to Do?* (London: Allen Lane, Penguin, 2009).

Sandel, Michael J., *A New Citizenship* (BBC Reith Lectures for 2009) <https://www.bbc.co.uk/programmes/b00kt7rg>, accessed 28 December 2021.

Shakespeare, William, *The Complete Works*, ed. W. J. Craig (London: Oxford University Press, 1905).

Skidelsky, Robert and Skidelsky, Edward, *How Much is Enough? Money and the Good Life* (London: Allen Lane 2012; Penguin, 2013).

Sobel, Dava, *Longitude* (London: Fourth Estate, 1996).

Sobel, Dava, *Galileo's Daughter: A Drama of Science, Faith and Love* (London: Fourth Estate, 1999).

Sobel, Dava, *The Planets* (London: Fourth Estate, 2005).

Spragens, Thomas A., Jr, *The Irony of Liberal Reason* (Chicago & London: The University of Chicago Press, 1981).

Suggate, Alan M., *William Temple and Christian Social Ethics Today* (Edinburgh: T&T Clark, 1987).

Suggate, Alan M., "The Temple Tradition", in Brown, Malcolm (ed.), *Anglican Social Theology: Renewing the Vision Today* (London: Church House Publishing, 2014), pp. 28–73.

Sumption, Jonathan, "Government by decree—Covid-19 and the Constitution", Cambridge Freshfields Annual Law Lecture, 27 October 2020. Transcript and video at <https://www.privatelaw.law.cam.ac.uk/events/CambridgeFreshfieldsLecture>, accessed 28 December 2021.

Sykes, Stephen and Booty, John (eds), *The Study of Anglicanism* (London and Minneapolis: SPCK/Fortress Press, 1988).

Tawney, R. H., *Equality* (London: George Allen & Unwin, 1931/1964).

Tawney, R. H., *Religion and the Rise of Capitalism: A Historical Study*. The Scott Holland Memorial Lectures for 1922, first published edition 1926 (Harmondsworth: Penguin Books, 1938).
Temple, William, *Personal Religion and the Life of Fellowship* (London: Longman's Green, 1926).
Temple, William, *Nature, Man and God* (London: Macmillan, 1934).
Temple, William, *Readings in St. John's Gospel* (London: Macmillan, 1939–40).
Thatcher, Margaret, *Speech to the General Assembly of the Church of Scotland*, 21 May 1988. Margaret Thatcher Foundation at <https://www.margaretthatcher.org/document/107246>, accessed 28 December 2021.
Thucydides, *The History of the Peloponnesian War*, tr. R. Crawley (London: J. M. Dent & Sons, 1910).
Volf, Miroslav, *Exclusion and Embrace: A Theological Exploration of Identity, Otherness and Reconciliation* (Nashville, TN: Abingdon Press, 1996).
Walker, Peter, "New appointment to stop spread of 'woke' culture on campuses", *The Guardian*, 15 February 2021.
Waterson, Jim, "Oliver Dowden: The paymaster who is calling the tune in the culture wars", *The Guardian*, 12 June 2021.
Welsford, A. E., *Life in the Early Church A.D. 33–313* (London: National Society and SPCK, 1951).
Whitworth, Patrick, *Three Wise Men from the East: The Cappadocian Fathers and the Struggle for Orthodoxy* (Durham: Sacristy Press, 2015).
Wilkinson, Richard and Pickett, Kate, *The Spirit Level* (London: Allen Lane, 2009/2010).
Williams, Rowan, *The Wound of Knowledge* (London: Darton, Longman and Todd, 1979, second, revised edition 1990).
Williams, Rowan, *Arius: Heresy and Tradition* (London: SCM Press, 1987, second edition 2001).
Williams, Rowan, *On Christian Theology* (Oxford: Blackwell Publishers, 2000).
Williams, Rowan, *Lost Icons: Reflections on Cultural Bereavement* (Edinburgh: T&T Clark, 2000).

Williams, Rowan, *Grace and Necessity: Reflections on Art and Love* (Harrisburg, PA and London: Morehouse-Continuum, 2005).

Williams, Rowan, *Faith in the Public Square* (London: Bloomsbury, 2012).

Williams Rowan, *Christ the Heart of Creation* (London: Bloomsbury Continuum, 2018).

World Council of Churches, *Baptism, Eucharist and Ministry*, Faith and Order paper 111 (Geneva: WCC, 1982).

Zuboff, Shoshana, *The Age of Surveillance Capitalism: The Fight for a Human Future at the New Frontier of Power* (London: Profile Books, 2019).

Index

This index is not intended to be comprehensive. Its primary aim is to enable the reader to explore the themes of this book.

abstract(ion)   7, 12, 51, 57–63, 69, 71, 90, 143, 156
adventurous(ness)   73, 158, 164
Aeschylus   69
Africa   iii, 43–4, 98, 157
Alexandria   113
alpha males   135
America(ns)   3, 27, 43–4, 75, 77, 157
Anglican(ism), Church of England   11–15, 79–84, 86, 125–7, 140, 157–9
Anglican-Roman Catholic *Agreed Statement*   126
Antioch   113
appetites   49, 60, 65, 72, 75
Aquinas, Thomas   31, 71, 86–8
Aristotle   27, 62, 71, 133
Arius, Arianism   110–11, 143
art, the arts   vi–vii, 1, 8, 28–30, 35, 47, 51–2, 61, 83, 85, 115
artificial intelligence   33
askesis   70–1, *see also* discipline
Athanasius   143
Attlee, Clement   18
Augustine, St   8, 11, 31, 78, 86–7, 106, 116, 119
authoritarianism   5, 88
authority   29, 35, 95, 139–41, 153
Ayer, A. J.   1

Bailey, Simon   14
Balthasar, Hans Urs von   89
baptism   12, 94, 98–102, 106, 115, 146, 148, 150, 169

barbarism   48
Barenboim, Daniel   46–51, 84, *see also* Said, Edward
Basil of Caesarea   71, 116, 144
Beethoven, Ludwig van   49–50
black people   43–4
Blair, Tony   19
body   7–11, 30, 58–62, 68–75, 85, 96, 122, 133–4, *see also* flesh, Incarnation, physical(ity)
body of Christ   12, 67, 70, 78–9, 84, 86, 93–7, 104, 106–9, 114, 118–21, 124–6, 145, 149, 152, 164, 168, 170, *see also* Church
Bonhoeffer, Dietrich   15, 137–40, 149–51, 156
Book of Common Prayer   13, 79, 122, 124
Bowra, C. M.   68
Bradshaw and Johnson   14, 107, 117–21
Breathing Space project   vi, 164–5, 167, 171
Brevint, Daniel   124–5
Brexit   4–5, 19, 41–2, 165
British Broadcasting Corporation   4, 32
Brontë sisters   73–4
Brown, Gordon   19
Brown, Malcolm   11, 86
Bunting, Madeleine   75–7

Caiaphas   138–9, 163
capitalism   2, 7, 18–19, 21–3, 33, 42, 77, 157–8, *see also* free-market, market

Cappadocia   71, 144
Carney, Mark   6–7
Catholic(ism)   15, 78, 88, 132, 164, see also Roman Catholicism
celebration   83, 126
Chalcedon, Council of   65–6
Chaplin, Jonathan   158
Charlemagne   117
children   8, 38, 43, 150
child sexual exploitation   38–9, 162–3
China   10, 42–3, 56–7, 99
Church   12, 27, 31, 65, 67, 82, 84, 86, 89, Part 3 passim, 142, 145–51, 157–8, 164, see also body of Christ
church buildings   115
Churchill, Winston   18
citizen(ship)   2, 21–3, 26, 29, 90
civil service   4, 32
climate emergency   3, 6, 24–6, 56–7, 135
coercion   140–1, 153, 170, see also power
colonialism   25, 42–5, see also imperialism
commodity, commodification   6, 50, 77, 90
common good, common life   6–9, 16, 21–2, 25–6, 29–30, 32, 40, 50–2, 82, 84, 90–1, 98, 132, 156, see also communal, individual, social
Common Worship   13, 126
communal, community   6, 22, 30–2, 35–6, 51, 59, 67, 71, 77, 82, 85, 90–1, 94, 96, 99, 126, 146, 149, 151, 153, 167, 169–71, see also common good, individual, social
communism   7, 48
competition   19–20, 23, 25, 83, 131, 136, 138, 141, 145, 149–51
Constantine   110, 113–15
Constantinople   110, 113, 115
Constantinople, Council of   65, 144
consumerism   20–23, 25, 29, 38, 48, 56
contemplation   46, 59, 70, 148
control   4, 19, 23, 25, 33, 58, 60, 62, 70, 75, 136, 138–9, 147
conversion   10, 67, 73, 125, 147–8
Corinth, Church at   95–7, 107–9, 118

Coronavirus, COVID-19   4–6, 25
cosmology   11, 58–9, 61–2, 64–5, 72–3, 132–4, 146
Cranmer, Thomas   122–6
creativity   36, 52, 73, 85, 145, 162, 164
Creator, creation   11–12, 62, 65–7, 69–70, 72–3, 83–90, 94, 102, 126, 130–7, 141–7, 149–53, 159, 163
Crockett, William   63, 122–4
cross, crucifixion   68, 93, 137–42, 145, 147–8, 153, 164, 166, 171
culture   6, 8–11, 15–16, Part 1, 56–7, 71, 76–7, 83, 85, 88, 94, 100, 117, 135, 156, 158–9
culture wars   6, 17, 44, 46, 52

Darwin, Charles   33–6
De Lubac, Henri   56, 86–9, 121, 156
Demant, Vigo   159
democracy   4–5, 21–2, 26, 32–3, 40, 45, 50, 57, 71, 81, 90
dependency   37, 132, 136, 141, 143, 145–6, 149, 151–3, 159
Descartes, René   7, 11, 28, 74–8
Didache   104
dignity, human   2, 18, 20, 26–7, 47
Diocletian   108–10
discipline   30, 35, 49, 52, 70, see also askesis
Dix, Gregory   12–15, 95, 104–23, 125–7, 130, 156
dogma   136, 147–8
Dowden, Oliver   44–5
drama   12, 57, 94, 145
dualism, duality   7, 10–11, 58–66, 69–84, 89, 96, 132–3, 152–3, 156–7, see also unity-in-diversity
Duffy, Eamon   119
Dura-Europos   115
dynamism   7, 29, 51, 70, 85, 88–9, 93, 134

economics   1–8, 18–25, 77, 81, 127, 135, 157
Ecumenical Movement   126
education   8, 48–9, 81
Edward VI   122

ekstasis   146–7
Elizabeth I   13, 79, 124
embrace   153, 160–5
emotion   1, 3, 5–9, 11, 36–7, 48, 75, 122
emotivism   1–8, 25, 27–32, 36–7, 42, 45–6, 49–50, 52, 80–1, 84, *see also* technocracy
ends and means   3, 8–9, 23, 26, 29–30
Enlightenment   2, 7, 11, 27–32, 37, 51–2, 73–5
environment   13, 24–6, 56–7, 76, 146, 149, 153
eros   146
eschatology   67, 84, 94, 97–8, 111, 114–15, 121, 127, 149–50
Eucharist, *see* Liturgy
European Union   4–5, 19, 40–2
Evangelicalism   124, 158
excellence   9, 30, 85
excess   51–2, 144
exclusion   136, 138, 153, 160–5
exorcism   100
experience   9, 17, 19–20, 29–30, 32, 39, 57, 60, 63, 65, 68–9, 71, 74, 142, 158, 162, *see also* life, ordinary

Facebook   33
faithfulness, fidelity   11, 139, 159, 163, 168
Fall, the   135–7, 145, *see also* sin
feel good   25, 49
financial crash of 2008   6, 19, 135
finite and infinite   131, 138, 140–3, 145–8, 151–3, 156
flesh   32, 61, 64, 67–8, 74, 93, 98, 130, 133, 149, *see also* body, Incarnation, physical(ity)
Francis, Pope   164
Frankopan, Peter   22–3, 40
free(dom)   1–2, 6–7, 21, 25, 33, 40, 42, 45, 47, 49–50, 64, 82, 136, 138, 141, 152, 163
freedom of God   89, 132–3, 136, 138–41, 148, 151–2
free-market, free trade   1–4, 18–24, 33, 42–3, *see also* capitalism, market
Friedman, Milton   2, 20–1

Galileo   37
Gaskell, Elizabeth   158
Germany   43, 79
gift   31, 66, 73, 83, 87–8, 96, 102, 108, 113, 130–2, 136–8, 141, 143–7, 152–3, 167–8, 171
Gnosticism   64–5, 69
God, *see* Creator, Jesus Christ, Spirit, Trinity
good life, the   8–9, 23, 26–30
Google   33
government   4–6, 17–18, 26, 33, 44–5
Graham, Elaine   37–8, 90–1
gratuitous(ness)   51–2, 85, 88, 132, 153
Greek/Graeco-Roman culture   31, 56–8, 63–5, 68–9, 98, 100, 105–7, 111, 115–16, 133, 143, 168
Greek Fathers   70–1, 86–9, 106, 124
Gregory III, Pope   117
Gregory Nazianzen   70–1, 144
Gregory of Nyssa   144
growth   19, 21, 23, 25

Hale, Lady   4
Harrison, John   37, 41
Hayek, Friedrich von   1–7, 20–1, 32, 84
Hebert, Gabriel   126
Hebrew/Jewish inheritance   31, 56–7, 63–6, 70–1, 82, 99–106, 113–14, 133–4, 136–7, 161, 163, 167–8
Helena, mother of Constantine   113
Henry VIII   79, 122
Higton, Mike   143–4, 156
history, historian   8, 10, 12–14, 30, 42–3, 45, 49, 67, 70, 77, 88–9, 97, 115, 134, 143–5, 150, 152–3
Hitler, Adolf   40, 79, 87, *see also* Nazism
holiness   68, 134, 148, 151
Hooker, Richard   123
hope   31, 39, 66, 69, 130, 143, 147
Hughes, John   11–12, 86
humanism   9–10, 17, 27, 38, 56, 87, 156
humanitarian(ism)   iii, 10, 80

human(ity), human nature 7, 9, 13–14, 28, 33, 38, 40, 48, 56–8, 61–2, 68, 72–3, 75, 80, 86–9, 130, 133–6, 140–7, 150, 152–3, 159, 169–70, *see also* person(al)

identity 8, 29–30, 32, 81, 85, 133, 136, 146, 153, 165
ideology 7, 20, 22, 32, 41–2, 49, 57, 81–2, 84, 159
image of God 69, 73, 83, 88, 133–4, 143, 145–6, 151, 153
imagination 36, 52, 61, 72, 83, 141, 147, 164
imperialism 6, 41–5, *see also* colonialism
Incarnation 64–5, 67, 69–70, 73, 80, 83, 89, 93–4, 102, 123, 137, 140, 142–4, 148, *see also* body, flesh, physical(ity)
India 42, 157
individual(ism) 1–2, 6–8, 10, 18, 20–1, 25, 28, 30–2, 39, 47–51, 57, 59, 77–84, 87, 90–1, 122, 124–6, 136, 141, 143, 157, 163, 165, 170–1, *see also* common good, communal, social
inequality, equality 2, 19–20, 22, 27, 41, 47, 80–1
integralist approach 11–12, 14–15, 48, 59, 86–91, 93, 107–8, 121, 125, 127, 132, 147, 156
integration 26, 47
integrity 6, 35, 52, 68, 81, 84, 87, 89, 96, 131, 134, 138–9, 141–2, 151–3
interdependence 47, 82, 149
Iona Community 126
Ireland 4
Irenaeus 13, 108
Islamic world 31
Ivison, Irene and Fiona 38

Japan 42–3, 91
Jarrow March 18
Jenkins, David 69, 143
Jenrick, Robert 44

Jerome 116
Jerusalem 96–8, 113, 115–16, 118, 137, 170
Jesus Christ 12, 31, 56, 64–7, 70, 82–3, 86, 89, 93–5, 97, 100–1, 106, 109, 112–14, 130–2, 137–53, 156–9, 163–4, 166, 168–71
John, St 64–6, 78, 88, 93–4, 105, 115, 137–9, 159, 166
John Chrysostom, St 166
John XXIII, Pope 86–7
Johnson, Boris, Prime Minister 5–6, 45
Jones, Simon 14, 130
judgment 67, 96–7, 130, 139–42, 147–8
judiciary 4, 32
Julia 99–104, 108
justice 2, 21, 24–5, 40, 74, 87, 127, 146, 148–50, 161
Justin 109

Kashgar 99
Kennedy, Robert 7–8
kenosis 140, 144–6, *see also* self-emptying
Kimber, John iii, 80
Kingdom of God 80, 94, 103–4, 107, 111, 114, 116, 125, 127, 138, 163–4
Kleeman, Jenny 38
Klein, Naomi 3
knowledge 1, 9, 28–31, 34–7, 49–52, 61–3, 70, 72–3, 85–6, 89, 94, 135, 141, 156, 158
Kuhn, Thomas 36

laity 90, 103–4, 112, 117–21
land 76–7, 138, 167–9
language, religious 40, 90, 130–1, 139, 148, 161
Lent, Jeremy 10, Part 2
liberal(ism) 1–3, 5–8, 21, 27–32, 36, 40, 90
life 4, 7–9, 12–13, 23, 31, 46–51, 65, 71, 73, 78, 83, 90–1, 93–6, 103, 105, 111–12, 130–2, 134–7, 142, 149–50, 153, 157–8, 162–4, 167, 170–1, *see also* experience, ordinary

limits   73, 131, 138–41, 153
Liszt, Franz   52, 171
Liturgical Movement   125–6
Liturgy   12–14, 70, Part 3, 130, 134, 163
Loach, Ken   20
Logos. logos   27–8, 64–5, 133–4, 137, 139–41, 145, 149, 158
Love, love   31, 52, 78, 80, 83–4, 88, 93–4, 107, 132, 136, 140, 143–53, 156, 162–5, 167, 170
Luke, St   97–9, 105, 107, 137–8, 160–5, 169

MacIntyre, Alasdair   3, 8–9, 29–32, 35, 39, 48, 51, 57, 85
MacLeod, George   126
Mark, St   105, 107
market   iii, 1–2, 6, 18, 20–2, 25, 33, 77, 90, 157–8, *see also* capitalism, free-market
martyrs   112, 114–15, 137
Marxism   7, 36, 87
material, matter   10, 57, 60, 68–9, 75, 132–3, 152–3
mathematics   1–2, 6, 9, 23–4, 28, 36, 51–2, 57, 59, 62, 72, 74
Matthew, St   iii, 105, 107, 137
Maximus the Confessor, St   15, 89, 133–4, 145–8
mediaeval period   56, 117–21
Milbank, John   89
mind   7, 11, 23–4, 26, 28, 68, 70, 72–6, 133–4
mindset   25, 31, 40
mission   57, 67, 89, 98–9, 109, 111, 125, 133, 150, 171
monasticism   71, 112–13, 118, 120
moralising/moralism   82, 157, 159, 162–4
moral(ity)   1–3, 7, 18, 28–9, 32, 39–40, 44, 59, 62, 75, 80, 83, 90, 125, 157–65
mortality   61, 114, 153
music(ians)   9, 30, 46–52, 59, 85, 94, 115, 171
muzak   48

mystery   13, 27, 89, 93, 95, 106, 109, 115, 126, 143–4, 171

narrative   26, 31, 42, 45, 47, 138, 147, 149–50, 167, *see also* story
Nathan the prophet   137
nationalism   4, 6, 24–5, 42
nature, natural world   10, 24–6, 28, 34, 38, 56–7, 59, 66, 73, 75, 135
nature and supernature   12, 59, 79, 86–9, 121, 152
Nazism   40, 47, 150, *see also* Hitler
Nicaea, Council of   65, 110–11, 143
nominalism   123

obedience   52, 100, 105, 109, 139, 145, 150
Olusoga, David   43
ordinary   7, 9, 12–13, 26, 40, 69, 94, 98–9, 107, 113–15, 118, 144, 153, 156, 162, 164, *see also* experience, life
Origen   70
Orphism   59
Orthodox Christianity   15, 40, 58, 89, 127, 132, 166
other(ness)   46–7, 135–6, 141, 146, 148, 153, 165, *see also* xenophobia
O'Toole, Fintan   41–2
ownership   22, 41, 76–7
Oxford Movement   125

Pandora Papers   5
Parliament   iii, 4–5, 13, 26, 32, 45, 79, 123
participation   27, 30, 49, 52, 63, 70, 78, 87–8, 96, 104, 106–8, 121–2, 125–6, 133, 146, 149
Pascha, Passover   101–3, 105, 114, 147
Paterson, Owen   32
patriotism   40, 83
Paul, St   11, 64–8, 74, 78, 93–7, 100–1, 108, 118–19, 133–4, 140, 149–50, 168, 170
Peacocke, Arthur   35–6, 76
Pentecost   97–9, 103, 114

perform(ance)   47–8, 51, 85, 94, 104, 121, 134, 162, 167
persecution   108–10
person(al)   6–11, 14, 25–6, 30–7, 52, 62, 69, 72–3, 76, 79, 82–3, 85, 88, 94, 96, 122, 126, 130, 133–4, 144–6, 151, 156, 158, *see also* human(ity)
perversity   8, 66, 72, 84, 135–7, 142, 163–4, 168
Peter, St   97–8, 114, 123, 142, 146
Philo   64
physical(ity)   8–9, 11, 28, 60, 64, 66–7, 72–3, 76, 118, 120, 133, *see also* body, flesh, Incarnation
Piketty, Thomas   22, 41
Pindar   68–9
Pius XII, Pope   86–7
Plato, Platonism   10–11, 27, 56–65, 69–73
play(fulness)   8, 52
Polanyi, Michael   9, 33, 35–6, 85
politics   3, 13, 21–2, 25–7, 29–30, 32, 45, 47, 50, 79–84, 116, 123
Polycarp, St   114
populism   5, 45, 48
poverty, poor   18–19, 71, 111, 170
power   3–5, 13, 28–30, 32–3, 45, 68–9, 81–2, 89, 93, 95, 104, 116, 120, 131, 133, 135–8, 140–3, 147–8, 150, 152–3, 169–70, *see also* coercion
practice, practical   8–9, 28–31, 34–7, 46, 51–2, 72, 85–6, 88, 90–1, 94, 96, 130, 132, 136
prayer   93, 100–4, 112–13, 117–18, 144, 148, 151
presbyters, priests   99, 102–3, 110, 117–21
Prodigal Son, parable of   15, 73, 160–5
projection   136, 141, 152
Protestantism   14–15, 75, 77–9, 132, 164
public and private   1–3, 8, 19–21, 28, 37–8, 58, 79, 90–1, 96, 109, 157–9
Puritans   75, 77
Putin, Vladimir, President   40
Pythagoras   59, 85

rationality, reason   1–10, 23, 25–32, 37, 42, 45–6, 52, 56, 59–60, 62, 72, 75–7, 85, 87, 90, 121, 133, 139–40, 146–7, 156, 158
receptionism   123, 126
reconciliation   11, 66–7, 88, 93, 148–50, 152, 162, 165
redemption   31, 68, 70, 72–3, 79–80, 84, 93, 101, 103, 111–12, 114, 126, 145, 159
Referendum of 2016   4, 19, 165
Reformation   79, 117, 121–2, 124, 137–8
relation(al)   11, 23, 26, 29, 39, 50, 66, 71, 73, 77, 83–4, 87–8, 96, 106, 125, 130–2, 134, 136, 142–5, 151, 160–5
remembrance (*anamnesis*), memory   iii, 40, 63, 76, 95, 102, 105–8, 114, 121–2, 126, 139, 160–1, 167–8
repentance   98, 147–8, 160
resurrection   66, 83, 89, 93–4, 101–2, 106, 114, 123, 133, 142, 147, 171
revelation   10, 148, 158, 166, 170
Rhodes, Cecil   44
Rogers, Nicholas   iii, 79–80
Roman Catholic(ism)   11, 14, 86–7, 117, 157, *see also* Catholicism
Rome   97, 113, 115, 117
Rowlands, Anna   157–8
Royal Supremacy   79, 123, 125
rule(s), regulations   21, 30, 49, 57, 61, 63, 161–4, 170
Russia   40

sacrifice   14, 68, 78, 105–6, 108–9, 114, 119–20, 122, 124–6
Said, Edward   46–51, 84, *see also* Barenboim, Daniel
saints' days   114–15
Sandel, Michael   22
Sappho   69
science(s)   1–3, 6–8, 13, 22–4, 27–30, 33–8, 49, 51–2, 56, 71, 76, 83, 85, 89
scientism   36
Scottish Clearances   77
scripture   100, 123, 138, 158, 168–9
Second Vatican Council   14, 87, 125

secular(ism)   14, 90, 149
security, insecurity   136
self-centred(ness)   72–3, 82, 146–7, 159
self-emptying, self-dispossession   52, 65, 130, 140–53, 170
sex robot industry   38
sexuality   65, 73–4, 78
Shakespeare, William   41, 135
Sharp, Granville   80
silence   46, 48, 148–9
sin   11, 64–8, 70, 72, 78–9, 83–4, 106, 112, 114, 140, 145–9, 153, 159, *see also* Fall
Skidelsky, Robert and Edward   8
slave(ry)   iii, 6, 43–6, 64–5, 67, 79–80, 95, 105–6, 111, 114, 153, 157, 160, 167
Sobel, Dava   37
social, society   2, 6–10, 18, 20–2, 26, 28–33, 47–51, 58–9, 68, 71, 80–5, 88, 90–1, 116, 125, 127, 130, 149–50, 158, *see also* common good, communal, individual
social media   3, 46
socialism   2–3, 18, 20
solidarity   7–8, 22, 82–3, 88, 140, 149–50, 169–71
soul   7, 10–11, 58–61, 69–70, 72, 75–6, 78–9, 83, 87, 91, 96, 133
sovereignty   5, 42
Spragens, Thomas   2–3, 27–9, 32, 45
Spirit, Holy   65, 73, 86, 93, 96, 100–3, 114, 120, 126–7, 144, 148, 164
spirit, human   7, 10–11, 13, 58, 72, 86, 133
Stalin, Joseph   40
state, role of   18, 58–61, 79, 81–2, 123
Stone, Kathryn   32
story   iii, 26, 38, 71, 73, 94, 99, 107, 144, 160–5, 167–8, *see also* narrative
subsidiarity   26
Sumption, Jonathan   4–5, 45
Sunday   113–14
Suor Maria Celeste   37
Supreme Court   4
surveillance   33

suspended middle   89, 152
suspicion   17, 44, 135–6, 138
symbols, symbolic thought   51, 57, 63, 70, 78, 85, 87, 94, 101, 106, 113, 123–5, 150
synaxis   94, 99–100, 112

Tawney, R. H.   27, 41, 157–8
tax, tax havens   18, 26
technocracy, technocrat   1–4, 7–8, 13, 23, 26–33, 36, 49, 52, 57, 80, 84, *see also* emotivism
technology, technician   10, 17, 22–4, 30, 33, 38, 40, 57, 85
Temple, William   11, 16, 56, 72, 82, 84, 86, 137, 141–2, 157–9, 166
Tertullian   109
Thatcher, Margaret, Thatcherism   2, 18–20, 22–3, 32, 80–4
Theodosius   116
time, temporal   9, 31, 49, 51, 63, 71, 85, 88, 93–4, 98, 111, 113–15, 130, 133, 135, 151, 167
tradition   26, 30–1, 35, 63–4, 86, 95, 101, 116–17, 132, 138, 158, 166
transformation transfiguration, transition   25–6, 68, 71, 90, 93, 130–1, 134, 146–7, 149–50, 153, 159
Trinity   11, 65–6, 72, 83, 86, 94, 130, 142–5, 151–3
trust   17, 20, 35, 136, 138, 147, 168–70
truth(fulness)   1, 3, 10, 15, 26, 28–9, 31–2, 40, 44, 51, 59–61, 71, 87, 89, 94, 141, 162, 169
Tyre   115

Ukraine   40
unemployment   18–19
unity-in-diversity   11, 50–2, 58–9, 63, 65, 67, 69, 72–3, 76, 83–4, 89, 93–4, 98, 104, 134, 148, 162, 164–5, *see also* dualism
utility, utilitarianism   1, 23, 26, 28, 52, 146

values   1–3, 6–8, 21–3, 25, 27–31, 75
Victorians   73–4, 158

violence   30, 136, 171
virtues   3, 8–9, 23, 26, 28–31, 70, 85
Volf, Miroslav   165

wealth   22, 26, 41, 83, 137, 150
Welsford, A. E.   14, 99
Wesley, John and Charles   124–5
wholeness   50, 68, 84, 142
Wilberforce, William   iii, 43
Wilkinson and Pickett   20
Williams, Rowan   14–15, 29, 51–2, 89, 127, Part 4, 156, 158
Windrush generation   44–5
wisdom   8, 35, 40, 60, 65, 82, 90, 95
women and men   37–8, 43, 64, 67, 73–4, 135, 138

work   83, 85, 113–14
world, universe   7, 12–13, 28, 51–2, 61–3, 65–6, 68, 76, 81–6, 89, 94–5, 108, 110–11, 130–4, 143, 145, 149–51, 156, 167
World Council of Churches   126–7
worship   12–14, 16, 69, 86, 90–1, 94–6, 98–100, 102–4, 108–9, 111–15, 130, 134, 148–50, 156, 168

xenophobia   47, 165, *see also* other(ness)

Zuboff, Shoshana   33

EU GPSR Authorized Representative:

LOGOS EUROPE, 9 rue Nicolas Poussin, 17000 La Rochelle, France

contact@logoseurope.eu

www.ingramcontent.com/pod-product-compliance
Lightning Source LLC
Chambersburg PA
CBHW070551160426
43199CB00014B/2461